WHAT DO YOU KNOW? IS IT REAL?

Authored By:

Ras Jah Strength

*

Quranic Scriptures (Ayats) provided by

Bro. Albert X

Copyright © 2014 by Solomon & Makeda Publishing

All Rights Reserved. No parts of this book may be reproduced in any form without the express written consent of Publisher/Authors, except in the case of brief quotations embodied within relevant articles and book reviews for print and electronic media.

Table Of Contents

PREFACE..i

INTRODUCTION...xiii

ABOUT THE AUTHOR..xvi

Chapter 1

THEME: SUBTLE PRESENCE- SUBTLE BEING...................1

Chapter 2

THEME: REVELATION IN DUTY...............................16

Chapter 3

THEME: INFERENCE IS MOVEMENT.........................34

Chapter 4

THEME: SELF-SEEKING SELF, SEEKING SELF...............45

ADDENDUM: COALESSING KNOWLEDGE...................66

EPILOGUE...110

GLOSSARY..112

Preface

What, may We ask, Is the purpose of the Sacred Scripts? Are they written just to fill Our Days with wonderful stories of events past? Are they revealed for one or any particular group, or are they teachings and explanations for everyone?

The Sacred Scripts, the Bible, Quran, Vedas, or whichever one or ones We know of, are Writings that summarize the Entirety of Life; so that We can use that Inspiration, that Knowledge, in Completing the Journey and Duties that We are obligated in fulfilling; on this Realm. As they stand, they themselves are completed works, but they aren't independent of each other. Rather, they are parts of an Intricate Matrix that isn't completely known or understood by those who profess to Love them. They are neglected, and in neglecting them We are neglecting Ourselves and the Preparation that We need to carry out before events begin to take place in Our Lives; because when they do, they will happen with that incompletion of preparation that We Created. With that being the case, We are then participating in a corrupted event, which will slow, stagnate, or freeze Our progress, just like a corrupt file can slow, stagnate, or freeze a computer.

We need to read All of Our Sacred Scripts; so that "Thought Seeds" are planted in Our Subconscious, and Conscious, Minds Giving Us the ability to, knowingly or even unknowingly, contribute to the events of Our Lives, and progress from them. We need to make sure that this happens no matter what, or We'll lose out on an opportunity to Succeed.

Each thought that We have needs to be completed. That is a necessity We can no longer afford to not do. We need to have, available to Us, mountains of information, knowledge, and wisdom; so that We can perform our duty in Life complete and proper. That means that all thoughts need to be recognized and determined. No more partial thoughts, ignoring thoughts and feelings, or even locking into a particular aspect of a thought. We must begin to observe, inquire, relate and satisfy each thought in its proper objectivity and entirety. But We can't do that from one, single, source.

It is a well-known fact that there are different ways, more comprehensive ways, to explain the same thing. Why is that? How can one system explain an aspect of something better than, or rather more comprehensively than, another? It could be that system's terminology, symbolism, doctrine, rituals, or a host of other things. Never-the-less, We just need to acknowledge that this is True, and then move on that Truth to acquire what We can from it. What We need to do is learn and learn constantly toward elevation. There should never come a time when We cease to learn, that would indeed be a day of mourning.

What Do You Know? Is It Real?

Most of Us are on a "Blind Journey," but what exactly is making "Us" Blind on this Journey? We are Blind on this Journey simply because We think that We have evolved instead of descended. We think that the Evolution from a Single Celled Organism, into a Multi-Billion Celled Species, is the Proper Order of Life. We do not know, nor believe, that We are in a True Degenerative State and Condition. That we are Spiritual Beings "Suffering" in the Flesh of this "Material" world. All of this is happening to Us because Our perception is not "Keen" enough to perceive the "Transient World Reality" that We are Truly a Resident of. The Subtle Characteristics of that Reality has no meaning to Us what-so-ever. We haven't considered, planned, or participated in, a Subtle Event in Our Entire Lives; and for those who do, We ridicule as strange or crazy. This is what keeps Us from developing any familiarity with Our Journey through Life. Our True Guidance and Directions are all of a Gnosis and Non-Eschatological nature, character, and type, that We need to know and operate within.

For Our Liberty to begin there needs to be a Keen Awareness of Subtle Activity developed. We Need to "Comprehend" "Subtle Guidance" and "Directions" wherever they may appear or derive from. A Re-Tuning to Our Former Observer Frequency of Spiritual Awareness will help Us create this Subtle Recognition through a system that skillfully exercises these necessary abilities, in which this work is also a contributor.

The Sense of Physical Attachment and Face Value Diagnosis has to become Nullified in order to Maximize Subtle Skills. We all contain in Us Inherent Spiritual Greatness. We are All Created and Formed in the Image and Likeness of God, Spiritually.

Within the Architecture of Our Image and Likeness is a Schema that propels itself from the depths of Our Essence, beyond Our flesh and bones, and enters Our Minds for Reasoning. These reasonings will be the considerations of the interpreted products of Innumerable Calculations that Micro-Logos makes in its Prescience for His participation.

We are given so much in Life. From the moment We are born, until the time in which We must depart, Information of all sorts, types, and conditionings bombard Our Senses and Captures Our Sense Perception; to the point of almost total annihilation of any other ability of Perception. We began to Concretize a mindset that doesn't allow for any change, renewal, or elevation, of Our Perception and Awareness Abilities.

Most of the Dis-ease We experience in Life is due to the mindset of rigidity. Life is a Free-Flowing Massive Entity of Forces and Energies that interconnect, interdepend, and interplay with one another. It is a constantly moving, changing, elastic fabric of unknown limits, and We are supposed to be a part of it; but being a part of such an elaborate, and pulsating, source of Energy, requires that We also possess and utilize the fabric of that source.

We are Created, Formed, and Made so that We are able to experience the totality of Our Source. This allows Us to come into existence and create a Reality comparable to "Life". When we do not Fully understand this, We Suffer. This is proven in the Eschatological teachings, mindsets, and ideologies that dominate most every society.

Yes, We are Suffering. We are Suffering because We think that We know, but We know not. We are Suffering because We are Afraid of knowing. We are Afraid of First Asking a Most Basic and Fundamental Question of Our Living.

We must ask this question because We must begin the process of removing what is not necessary for experiencing Life in the most purified manner, first in an individual perspective, and secondly in Our Collective Ideal. That question is, "Quidest Veritas" "What Is Truth"?

What Is Truth is a vague and obscured question. Most would say that truth is unchangeable, fundamental, reality, logical, insurmountable, instrumental and almost every other subjective phrasing. The dictionary defines truth as being faithful, constant, sincere, fact, even transcendent. It refers one to True, which says it is faithful, sure, steadfast, loyal, in accordance with actuality, fully realized, that which is the case rather than what is manifest or assumed, consistent, legitimate, you get the picture. But, what all of these terms and phrases say is only relative to the ones who agree with whichever one they agree with. To everyone else, that term or phrase may be erroneous. Depending on who one asks, and where their comprehension of truth is derived, religious or secular, their answer may not be so simple, not clear. For the Truth is elusive in this world. It is of such a high esteem that homo sapien's commonality is almost an insult to it. It is simple, but the simple has become complex to the minds that relish in human suffering. It seems that the more our brains evolve, to higher and higher cognitive functions, the more we make the simple more difficult to comprehend and understand. It has become desirable, nowadays, to design complexities of the simple; in order to show some assumed advancement in the thoughts and thinking of mankind. But Truth is neither objective or objectifiable. It itself has no complexities, and any attempt to do so to Truth, objectify it or add complexness, is conjecture, and is then only transferring a lie and falsehood to those who are an audience of that presentation.

    In actuality, Truth can't even be explained truthfully. There are no words that can capture and define this Highest Form of Reality. All that is being done in explanation is synonymous with road signs to a particular destination. The Destination is beyond the reality of any sign that points to it. Just think of a sign pointing out the direction to the beach. In no way, shape, or form is that sign ever remotely similar to the actual beach. So it is with Truth, and what it Is.

What Do You Know? Is It Real?

In order to be a Truth all areas, and every aspect of Life, have to be satisfied by its applicability. There are no exceptions to the rule with Truth. Truth is the exception to man's rules. No one can give away Truth or make it so absolutely clear that the world sees it for what it is.

Truth is an inner working, fundamental, screen for projection, projector, synergistic, reflective, revealing Entity. It has operational functions that are similar to gravity, in the sense that it can attract or propel an observation, acceptance, or comprehension. It can stir one to emulate or create a petrification in the development and advancement of one that it has come into some form of interaction with.

Truth calls for a Self-Evaluation, Introspection, Analysis and overstanding of what may be lacking in one who is comprehending of it. Our egos constantly compare Us to any information that we may take in; and it does this more so than any other time when that information is a Truth.

How does one identify a Truth in his or her awareness? Well, based on the simple measure of community normalities, a Truth will most likely be all or in part contradictory to any commonalities we accept and practice. Compared to a ridgid way of living, a Truth can even be obscene to one who has become aware of it. It is why some people vehemently deny and fight against the Truth as it is compared to their ready-made world of deception.

The Truth has no compromising element or ability. It is either for or against that in which it has observed, investigated, evaluated and concluded, as either valid or non-valid, in an Elevational Analysis. The Truth exenterates past illusions of necessities and extirpates them from True Reality.

If one asked One's Self "Quid est Veritas," What is Truth, he or she, them or they, would have to repeat this question every day, and seek its overstanding till every night. A seeker of Truth makes seeking Truth the one constant in their life, never deferring or detouring from it. Life and all its activities become the machinery that drives them, give them energy, support their causes, and keeps them strong.

Truth, being relative, absolutely gives it a natural and transcendental character. It allows Us to accomplish so much by having this twin fold nature. Having a growing overstanding of Truth permits that ease of accepting so much of life; that We may not fully agree with at that time. It helps Us in our adaptation and evolution as human beings. How and where We are today is indicative of this fact, and never have We been ever more seeking than We are right now. We are at the cusp of overstanding some of the deepest, most ancient, of mysteries about our universe; and that has Us fast forwarding to the next question We can answer.

Let Us make a declaration here and now. Truth, and what it is, is not hiding, nor is it ever hidden from anyone to know. It is always there, ready and willing to be recognized. But, what happens to its being known is Our inability to look further, reach higher, and dig deeper, with Our minds, in order to see what is available to Us. We have to develop our ability to strip away derivatives & divaricates and enucleate Truth for a clear, unobstructed, perception of all that can be comprehended of it, in the area of Our concern. If not, We will continue to make the mistake of using erroneous conclusions in solving the problems and circumstances of everyday life.

You see, Truth is not just something We can use to solve major macrocosmic problems. Truth should function as an operating system in Our everyday lives. Truth has no limit, except the one that We impose on it. Truth is extremely acute and penetrating; if allowed the time to fully engage the circumstance. Knowing that most of the world's ideas are obstinate and obdurate, it is imperative to contact Truth and bond with it; so that the undulation between subject and object doesn't hinder a realization of what is observed, and applicable, to Our situation or circumstance.

In mathematics, specifically geometry, there are two terms describing angles and their totality of degrees, complementary and supplementary, that when one solves for the missing degrees reveals a Truth that already existed prior to even the question. So by this example, and many others to come, We can say that Truth is not some created thing, but an existing thing of its own origin, within reality.

The reason We cannot grasp Truth in higher realms, resulting in an elevation, is because, at this point, in the evolution or devolution of man, We have become severely myopic in vision; with no ability to detect this condition in Ourselves or Our species. We are truly Spiritual Beings, but We have mastered the role of being Man to the point where We are ostentatious in being man. That leads to the "Creation of Karma", which takes Us down deeper and deeper into the devolution of Our spiritual nobility and royalty.

This ostentatious mindset has programmed man to be a diffusionist (an anthropologist, in which We all are,) while never really being concerned as to Truth in its origin, as it truly is, but rather in branches, versions, episodes, and exfoliates that man pass off as "True". The diffusionist mindset is where the real Self-Harm is. It is the focus on what is different and why instead of what is similar, common, and why.

The Truth has a Rule, has a Kingdom that it exists in, that does not diminish, weakens, or alters in what it is. It is girded with its sword upon its thigh and is Most Mighty. None is stronger or has power over it. The Sword of Truth is one of Glory and Majesty, and while maybe these words seem religious or spiritual, they accurately describe how We should revere Truth in an applicable mental state.

Truth is, and has, a Throne of Representation. It's one that extends through time and space. Opposite its sword, is the scepter; revealing the jewels of high rights and responsibility, the quintessentials of attributes that calls upon the seeker.

Truth has to manifest, out of eternity, for the revealing and founding of what's Wonderful, Counselling and Mighty towards man, and his need of elevation. It is Parenting, a Father of internal, peace, and serenity. A Prince to the youthful, in development and maturation.

Truth's hierarchy position is King of Kings, Lord of Lords, Fact of Facts. Truth sets up what would be a Kingdom, which shall never be destroyed. Truth's Kingdom cannot be invaded or left to any other people, as other so-called Kingdoms can, and It only shall stand forever. None can resist, flee, defend, or overcome this plight of theirs. Truth and Truth alone is Eternal, Infinite, and it is Truth's essential nature in being so.

Truth cometh, and is just, having salvation from a world of injustice, inequality, prejudices, biases, and wrongdoings, towards the innocent and righteous seeking. The humility and lowly entrance that Truth uses is mocked as not having power and authority. Oh, what a mistake of judging from the outside, and not even considering what is internal, and essentially, the Reality of what has manifested. A witness to the people, a leader and a commander to the people is what has come forth and is the establishment of Truth.

Before We get into the in-depth purpose of this writing, We want to explain a foundational aspect of Our current "Point of References". Our Koine Ennoiai (GK), or Common Sense, which is Our fundamental ability to perceive, understand, and judge things, has bestowed on Us a system we call "Coalescing Knowledge"; that We wish to share with Our Brothers & Sisters. We hope to create a "Common To", in Our People, that can, from this day forward, be expected of nearly everyone without any need to debate.

We are One species, One type. There are no other types of Homo Sapiens here right now. We Function the same, within the similar circumstance of Our Basic Fundamental Needs. So why do We think that We think differently when it comes to Religion, Politics, or Social Standards? God is Single, His Ways are Single, and the Way to Him is Single. Our Applications may be different because Our Lives are different, but when We continue to "Apply Truth," We will find that We are in Similitude with One Another.

This Similitude has been observed by Us through Our Common Sense of Coalescing Knowledge. We have discovered the "Truth Intent" of the Sacred Scripts and their Inspiration. With that in Mind, We move to use All Sacred Scripts, every Science, and any Knowledge available, that will assist Us in Performing Our Duty, of Being Who We Are, and What We Are, to Our People. Beginning with the studious knowledge gained from the Holy Bible and Holy Quran, and common information gained from Psychiatry, Psychology, and Social Science.

Introduction

What Do You Know: Is It Real? Is a look into Our individual, and sometimes collective, psychology, sociology, anarchy, oligarchy, thinking, feeling, seeing, realizing, and overstanding. It touches on ideologies, philosophies, conspiracies, and what is considered to be advancements in science and technologies that affect the human being. It brings up what is interesting within Our identity, appearance, reflection, and self-detection. There is a lot going on with us, at any given moment. What Do You Know: Is it Real? Is an introductory journey into the universe of what we "Do Not Know" about Ourselves?

What Do You Know: Is It Real? Is also an intriguing beginning of Our Self-Discovery, Self-Knowledge, and Self-Improvement. It seeks to "Reveal" the operations of Our "Background" selves, and introduces what can be established as a working connection to Our Reality. In this "Revelation", it points out that there is something more going on than what meets the eye.

Everything that We express can be attributed to the psycho-historical, psychogenic modes, that We were reared in as children. These six psycho classes: Infanticidal, Abandoning, Ambivalent, Intrusive, Socializing, and Helping, and to what degree any one or multiple/combination were used, concretized everything that we know, and feel is Real about life and what we experience in it. These childhood and adolescent experiences determined what social facts we would adhere to, psychiatric disorders, from psychoses to neuroses, that we could suffer, or are prevented from suffering, are how would our metacognition: cognition about cognition, thinking about thinking, knowing about knowing, becoming aware of our own awareness, and higher-order thinking skills, would operate when attempting to use particular strategies for learning and/or problem-solving. What Do You Know: Is It Real? Will light up this opened, Elephant sized, "Pandora's Box" that is either being ignorantly ignored or is illiterately unknown.

Maleficent social behaviors like prejudices, crimes, discriminations, and even wars are all self-destructive re-enactments of earlier abuse, neglect, and injuries, that we subconsciously flash-back to, in decision making and responded to in perceived aggression, from earlier fears of Our Destructive Parenting; that dominated previous individual and social behaviors. So, while we may see advancements in some areas of society, the underlying issues that plagued Our Ancestors, fore parents, and parents, still exist, because of their never being addressed and healed. And having never received any therapy, counseling, or rehabilitation, has only allowed these conditions to worsen.

In Our worsening we have suffered from Negative Unconditioned Responses (the unlearned response that occurs naturally in reaction to the unconditioned stimulus); Negative Conditioned Response (the learned response to the previously neutral stimulus); Destructive Social Cognitive theories (the portions of an individual's knowledge acquisition that is directly related to observing others within the contest of social interactions, experiences, and outside media influences); Corrupted Observational Learning (learning that occurs through observing the behaviors of social models such as parent, sibling, friend, teacher, particularly in childhood, or someone of authority or higher status); and Mired Classical Conditioning (a learning procedure in which a biologically potent stimulus is paired with a previously neutral stimulus. After paring is repeated, the organism exhibits a conditioned response to the stimulus). These psychological tools and mechanisms have become weapons of Mass Destruction; used in every category of society to hinder, upset, neutralize, corrupt, and eliminate a melanistic people from any respected position in civilization. But unlike any primordial or proclivical response, these weapons must be acquired through experience, and are relatively impermanent, therefore, able to be removed.

Our melanistic people suffer from a fear induced, perceived threat of terror by the Stimulus Generalization of Mankind, and especially Europeans. Fear is one of the most common, classically conditioned, responses experienced by humans, and this has become Our syndrome.

About the Author

Whatever is accomplished is done so with an agreement between those involved, and This work is no exception. Two men, who became brethren through a beckoning of their "Ultimate Reality", crossed paths that began a coalescing of seemingly distant "Ways of Life". A Nation of Islam Muslim and a Rastafari Priest would not appear to exist in the same effect, at first thought, but beyond sighting shows that the things aren't always what others hope they would be.

There're two places in life that can bring men together; in an effort to create change. One of those places is their past, the other is their future.

Bro. Albert X and Ras Jah Strength came together for the future of "Our People". They were brought together by prayer and faith and are maintained as brethren through the same. They coalesce and strive within the teachings of the God of Abraham. This is their foundation. That is their strength.

Both are from Miami. Both sustained the blow of the United States of America's Department of Justice. Both survived the Federal Bureau of Prisons. And both, with All Praises Due To The Most High, are striving for the Betterment of themselves and Our People.

Leaders, with the attributes of the Spiritual and characteristics of Love. Committed to the success and Victory of our cause, toward the elevation of the people. Appreciating the Life we all share as divine.

This was the Energy that inspired this book. I was smitten by this potent Brotherhood to reveal my thoughts and overstandings. It is my prayer that you gain a variety of "New Visions" that quicken your Spirit and revitalize your Life.

Ras Jah Strength

Chapter 1

Subtle Presence – Subtle Being

Subtle. Even the spelling and pronunciation is not a clear concise thing. I mean, what is the deal with the "B" in the middle that most of us are taught not to strongly articulate? This ambiguity of that letter "B" speaks to what subtle defines. It is not a concrete thing, even though it exists here. It is also not a purely imagined or imaginary thing either. What subtle speaks to, I suggest, is "reality potential", that which is and possibly can also be. How can this suggestion be true or accurate? Well, we would have to take a page out of physics where it explains the Collapse Wave Principle of a particle. In this explanation, a particle is at first everywhere, which makes it also no-where in particular. But once observed, it's everywhere wave existence collapse into a particular objective existence observable for that moment. So it is with the subtle. We are defining the subtle as being out there, everywhere, waiting to be observed and grasped, and when it is, what it produces becomes part of our living, existing, manifested world.

Subtlety comes from a transcendent domain of super consciousness. It manifests the ideals of subjectivity and couples them to an objective design, time and motion. An analogy of this would be baking a cake. The idea of baking a cake is not in any place that one can see, feel, taste, or touch, but yet it comes into our minds. Then the ingredients have to be brought in from wherever they might be and whatever they might be. Proper proportions are measured and mixed until they are consistent with what they should be, based on that ideal. Another process allows for the ingredients to become more of a single entity until "tadaa" we have a cake. All of this comes together from great distances for the sole purpose of being a cake. So does everything in all of existence operate. We just don't realize it.

The subtle is imminent. It's not like it itself comes forth, but it produces that which does, through its mechanisms and devices. It lies outside of space-time. Explained by Aristotle, when defining what matter is in its essence (subtle): "in abstraction, also, the potential substance upon which form acts to produce realities". The subtle is just that, it has no form or body to speak of, but yet it is a major element or component of bodies.

The subtle is a "Nascent" of all things. It doesn't ask for permission to exist or even exist because of something. The subtle lies where time and space itself is oblivious and nothing is beyond its influence.

BIBLE REF. KJV (1) GEN. 3:1; (2) JOB 1:6; (3) EPH. 6:11

GENESIS 3:1

Now the serpent was more subtle than any beast of the field which the Lord God had made. And he said unto the woman…"Ye shall not surely die"…

JOB 1:6

Now there was a day when the sons of god came to present themselves before the LORD, and Satan came also *among* them.

EPHESIANS 6:12

For we wrestle not against flesh and blood, but principalities, against powers, against the rulers' darkness of this world, against spiritual wickedness in high places.

HOLY QURAN (1) 2:34; (2) 7:11-18; (3) 15:26-44

CH. 7 THE ELEVATED PLACES VERSES 11-18

Section 2: The Devil's Opposition to Man

[11]And We indeed created you, then We fashioned you, then We said to the angels: Make submission to Adam. So they submitted, except Iblis; he was not of those who submitted. [12]He said: What hindered thee that thou didst not submit when I commanded thee? He said: I am better than he; Thou has created me of fire, while him Thou didst create of dust. [13]He said: Then get forth from this (state),

for it not for thee to behave proudly therein. Go forth, therefore, surely thou art of the abject ones. ¹⁴He said Respite me till the day when they are raised. ¹⁵He said: Thou art surely of the respited ones. ¹⁶He said: As Thou has adjudged me to be erring, I will certainly lie in wait for them in Thy straight path,¹⁷ Then I shall certainly come upon them from before them and from behind them, and from their right and from their left; and Thou wilt not find most of them thankful. ¹⁸He said: Get out of it, despised, driven away. Whoever of them will follow thee, I will certainly fill hell with you all.

CH. 15 THE ROCK VERSES 26-44

Section 3: The Devil's Opposition to the Righteous

²⁶And surely We created man of sounding clay, of black mud fashioned into shape. ²⁷And the jinn, We created before of intensely hot fire. ²⁸And when they Lord said to the angels: I am going to create a mortal of sounding clay, of black mud fashioned into shape. ²⁹So when I have made him complete and breathed into him of My spirit, fall down making obeisance to him. ³⁰So the angels made obeisance, all of them together. ³¹But Iblis (did it not). He refused to be with those who made obeisance. ³²He said: O Iblis, what is the reason that thou art not with those who make obeisance? ³³He said: I am not going to make obeisance to a mortal, whom Thou hast created of sounding clay, of black mud fashioned into shape. ³⁴He said: Then go forth, for surely thou art driven away. ³⁵And surely on thee is a curse till the day of Judgment. ³⁶He said: My Lord, respite me till the time

when they are raised. ³⁷He said: Surely thou art of the respited ones. ³⁸Till the period of the time made known. ³⁹He said: My Lord as Thou hast judged me erring, I shall certainly make (evil) fair-seeming to them on earth, and I shall cause them all to deviate, ⁴⁰Except Thy servants from among them, the purified ones. ⁴¹He said: This is a right way with Me. ⁴²As regards My servants, thou hast no authority over them except such of the deviators as follow thee. ⁴³And surely hell is the promised place for them all. ⁴⁴It has seven gates. For each gate is an appointed portion of them.

In these scripts Holy Bible (KJV): Gen. 3:1; Job 1:6; Eph. 6:11. Holy Quran: 2:34; 7:11-18; 15:26-44 there is a subtle, sublime, existence with a human present perception.

What is man, demon, jinn, angel except for subtle revelations of a hidden Realm of Mind. We are concerned with these concepts because they reflect a truth that we haven't yet mastered. That truth is that Satan, Lucifer, the Devil, is within us, as a part of us, revealing desire to us in different degrees, and we are confronting this object without considering the subtle subjectivity of that object. Satan is our adversary or antagonist, but his opposition is of an internal origin and conclusion. There is nothing outside of us that creates this conflict. It is a self-derived, individual, production of an experience that most of us unknowingly choose to be a part of.

Most teachings will have us to believe that Satan, demons, or a jinn comes up and tempts us, from the external, with an external object. But the truth of the matter is, and always was, that Satan is only an accuser of what we ourselves desire secretly. This accuser points out any weakness that is found to now be of a great threat to our decision making and well-being. It's pointing these things out as a real and progressive service to us. But since we aren't taught that, we only see it as a disservice. So we call it temptation instead of observation or even diagnosis.

Imagine if the subtleness of the dragon wasn't revealed as a simple serpent in Genesis, but as a dragon who is also a serpent. The next obvious question by us would naturally be "How can he be both", and that would open up the subjective door of conceptualization and explanation. And trust me, a red creature with horns and some type of pitchfork weapon, with a menacing smile, would be the furthest thing from our minds.

Satan is not a physical entity, at least not in the tangible sense that substances materialize in this manifested world. It is a thought, it is mental, psychological, spiritual, subjective, metaphysical, incorporeal, discarnate, and asomatous.

What do you do with your thoughts? What do you do with your memories? What do you do with the electrical pulses that cause body functions, muscle movements, and actions? I already know, and now you should know that you do nothing with these, or rather, you do nothing with the origin of these. What a terrible waste. You see, to understand the subtlety of worldly things is to fully recognize their benefit or injury to us. We need to know, recognize, and understand where all of our thoughts, memories, and electrical pulses come from and are going. These are very informative aspects of ourselves that we barely, if at all, use. This is why so much programming can be done to us, and we won't even know that it's being done. This is why we don't overstand anything that is spoken about in a spiritual or subjective way. We have distanced ourselves from the observational position of the source, that we once had, to a simple glimpse of the object that appears in a rudiment form. In Genesis 3:1 we are told of the subtlety of the serpent. But, what we do not ask or infer is where is this subtlety taking place, and what is the origin, and the destiny, of it? These are important questions that would service our lives in resplendent ways.

    The subtle is where the announcement of action derives from. It is here that not just what we do but how we do it begins to form. The subtle is where the assimilation of our entire history becomes real in our current lives. It is why words like accident and coincidence are only lies about why an event has happened, because its origins are unthinkable to us. We cannot continue to supply ourselves with the erroneous answers to all the decision we make.

    Let me tell you just how confused, backward, and ignorant we really are concerning our lives and the world that we live in. We are self-aware, self-realizing beings. That indication alone means that we play a critical role in the creation process. We create within creation itself, and we don't know this, or aren't fully aware of this ability.

Now it is said of our Archetype that He only need say "Be" and it is. So in what other way does our being made in His "image and likeness" of is there for us to create other than saying "Be" and it is also? Let me help you out, there is no other way. In the exact same way that the Creator Creates, He endows us with that same ability. It's not as grand, I'll admit, but it is done in the exact same way. Not knowing this in the most full and realized way is causing a manufacturing of the most degrading, insulting, corrupted, offensive, dehumanizing, and beastly of events in our lives, and the lives of those in the company of us. We are not realizing that it is not the clean version of our thoughts, that we actually announce, that are being produced, but every thought is being produced. We are producing what we need and don't need. We are producing the good, the bad, and the ugly of this world all because us and our thoughts are running wild, running madly out of control.

Do you really think that no one knows your thoughts or intentions; that you do not express them in some other ways? Do you think that they all come up only in you and that you have a barrier that prevents them from moving on or outward? Let me give you the results of a little experiment done to prove this position.

The experiment had pregnant women sing nursery rhymes to their babies during the first 32 to 34 weeks of pregnancy. They recorded the mothers to be as they sung to their babies. Four weeks later, at the 38th week, they played the recorded version instead of the real mother's voice and got the same response in the babies' heart rate as they did when the moms sang it themselves. Now if a child, with the most limited of its abilities, can realize the intent of the recorded version of those nursery rhymes, from the mother, doesn't that speak to the depth of our thinking, and how we don't yet fully comprehend it? From that stimuli the child created the only scenario it knew, at that time, which was a similar heart rate, it made its own world from the mother's thinking.

But what happens as the years pass by? Well, we begin to take on so much information, so much confusion, so many lies; a lot of deceit, malice, and corruption, that we do not, or cannot properly calculate the adjustments needed to find and secure a balanced state. We begin to answer one circumstance and before we complete it we begin on another, and another, and another. We combine so many thoughts that don't belong together, and in that process, we create a "Frankenstein Thought". A thought that is pieced together, and not even from our best thinking, but from a lot of incomplete thoughts. It becomes some nasty, horrible existing thing that we cannot recognize, so we say that life is being hard on us, or that God is trying us in the fire, or even that Satan is tempting us, when none of that is accurate or true. We are experiencing what we are experiencing of our own doing. We are experiencing what we are experiencing simply because we don't know or understand that we are creators, and we don't know or understand the creation process.

Everything and I do mean all things, are products of our own intimate thinking. It has always been this way, and it will always be this way.

Every scenario that you are placed in is based on your thinking prior to that event. It could have been a thought you had a few seconds ago or a thought that you had twenty years ago. Nevertheless, it is yours, and you created it.

Your thinking is out of control; Your creating is out of control; So, your life is out of control. Don't go looking around for the problem, unless you're looking for a mirror to look into. When it comes to creating, and the creation process, your thoughts are what's giving you the life that you are living. Do you think that the creation process differentiates between your so called good thoughts and your bad thoughts? All it knows is that you thought it, so you must want it. Your problem is that "YOU" don't know the difference between them. You get, want, and need all mixed up in definitions; You place desires before needs; And you love others but hate yourself. How in the devil do you think anything good can come from that mind, that would be impossible. I am telling you this so you can really feel what's going on with you, so you can do something about it. Quit bringing suffering into your life so you can suffer. Turn your misery around, because you thinking miserable is causing you to be miserable. If you have any thought, consciously take it towards a betterment of yourself. Think to yourself, "How can this thought be helpful", "What can I use this thought for that would be positive", "Where can this thought work properly towards life." If you do this, you can make your life and your world a beautiful place to "Be." Be in control of what is going on in and around you.

It is why you must guard your mind of all the information that is coming into it. The baby created a harmonious state because that's the only state it knew. You have to "only know" a harmonious state also. You have to discipline yourself so that no matter what happens you create a harmonious state that will be expressed externally. You have to slow your thinking down so that you complete all of your thoughts in their fullness; no more creating Frankensteins. This doesn't require maturity, but infancy. You have to become born again so that you can maintain your infant equipoised state permanently. No matter the initial thought continue to create it into a pure, harmonious, innocent thought that's complete. No more mixing of incomplete thoughts. The only thoughts that should be brought together are the ones that can coalesce into something very special for you.

There is no G.P.S. coordinates that point to a particular place that the Sons of God go to meet Him and divulge what they have been doing. That's why we also cannot locate the Mystical Garden of Eden. These representations point us inwards in a direction we have yet to look. They're not places to go or be at geographically, but places to go or be at subtly; in the realm of mind. The true definitions of these places can only be determined there, in our mental and psychological states, our subtle existence, in our hearts and minds. This is the only way an infinite and eternal being can fully exist. Outside of the inner realm is all sorts of limitations that cannot be attributed to an infinite existence in an eternal realm. Chaos reigns here. Destruction and decay are all around us. From the most distant star, in the most distant galaxy, in the most distant part of our universe to the paper, ink, and words that you are now reading, all will eventually come to an end as material existence. You nor anyone else will be able to find it in any other place outside of the subtlety of an inner realm of life.

In using an explanation from one of the scholars on this subject, Descartes, for example, said that the only thing whose existence seemed directly certain was man's consciousness, or mind, and so 'subject' came to designate the conscious mind and 'subjective' what belonged to it. If our own mental activity is the only unquestionable fact of our experience, all our knowledge may be called 'subjective', and views which start from this position may be called 'subjectivist'.

In this day and age, we can no longer choose to be either diachronic or synchronic. It is necessary to be both, as well as calculated, broad, scientific, thorough, and in-depth, concerning the things that are known, so that the infinite backdrop to that known thing can reveal itself in historical grandeur and contemporary expression.

Comprehending the subtle or subjective is not to eliminate what is physical or manifested, on the contrary, it's the physical and manifested that should be used in order to find the directions towards the subtle and subjective. Without the physical representation, one will not know the deeper, higher things. This knowledge of the subtle can only be gained when the signs and symbols of the manifested world began to speak and make sense. The subtle isn't gained to comprehend through a void or a vacuum, it is attained because of what it manifests and produce when we interact with that which is manifested.

Mastering of the physical world creates a connection between the subtle and physical. If one was to lean too much on one or the other he will be in grave danger of losing himself in a conflict of his reality, and the state of condition that his mind will have would be in error. There is no explanation truly sufficient enough to satisfy the subtle without the physical or the physical without the subtle. Through the Tree of Life system of explaining, the four trees that come from the Divine to the manifested, we learn how and that the subtle becomes the manifested. In physics, the subtleness of particles become atoms, which in turn become elements that manifest physically.

God Himself doesn't do anything in this world unless it is manifested by the hands of man. His description of Life, and Life more abundant, is thought by Him subtlety, and then He reveals it physically. This is truly the Fullness of Life, or else, what is it that we are to think about? Are we to think that only one limited aspect of either the subtle or the physical is real? Heaven forbids, Science forbid, both say that the two are necessary and that one depends on the other for completeness and a satisfactory explanation.

Think of "Spiritual Wickedness" and even further "Spiritual Wickedness in High Places"? Here we are being taught of a wickedness that is beyond the physical aspect that we are familiar with. This is suggesting that the true strength and power of wickedness is in the spiritual, intangible state. Look at how spiritual, a word many ascribe to mean righteous, is used here as an adjective describing what type of noun, in wickedness, we have. This is saying to us that this knowledge is a knowledge that can deceive one into thinking that what is perceived is good. It can heal, protect, provide and many other services that would render the observer unaware of its true intention. "In High Places" is another perspective that identifies to what degree this Spiritual Wickedness actually operates.

The "High Places" is none other than our subjective, subtle world. We have falsely given our manifested world the title of being real when in actuality it isn't. The "High Places" are real, the High Places are the areas that need our authoritative attention. It is in the High Places that the subtle begins its march across the great plains of our minds. This is our true Nascent and eternal existence.

Where can we find or locate principalities? Can we determine the ability and force of power? Do we have any idea about the "Rulers of the Darkness of this World"? If you can physically appropriate these in any fashion, then you are truly in lack. For these concepts and ideas are positioned in a state that no man's hands can ever manipulate. We cannot bring these down to the manifested level. These are of those things that we must elevate up to.

    Elevating up to the subtle is exactly what is being done in the verses and ayats that speak of Satan and Man being in the presence of one another. In the Quran, it says that Iblis (Satan) refused to make obeisance or submit to man. His reason was that he felt that he was better than man, being made of from fire, which made him subtle. But in truth, if Iblis would have raised up his subtle awareness he would have seen that he was not making obeisance or submitting to man, but to the will of God. For it was God who, based on the Quran, told Iblis to make obeisance or bow before man. So even Satan, who is subtle, fails, based on the narratives, to recognize a source's subtlety. And as for Man, who was formed from sounding clay, who is a reflector of what is perceived by him, he needs to observe what and where is it that he is reflecting from and towards. Without this keen observation, Man will never acquire the maximum application of his total potential, for Satan lies in wait in the straight path.

2

Revelation In Duty

    The Revelation definition that is to be understood here is a definition that speaks to the root of this particular spelling, and that is *Revel*. To revel is to have pleasure or delight in. This pleasure or delight comes from the earnest asking or the earnest desire to do right in the sight of God and man. Beginning with revel allows for a higher sense of purpose to take flight towards the revealed and what one may perceive.

    Man moves, all the time, with the hope or assumption that he will receive a reward or benefit from his actions. But just think about this, when have we ever had to know something before we committed the action that possibly would produce the results that we were hoping for? And who realizes, or apprehends fully, what a single act will bring forth; let alone a multiple-step plan that has so many human variables attached to it? It is a Reveling in the possibility that directs man's decision, and blindly, man begins to stir. No one knows or accepts that they are really moving on Blind Faith, but we are. With the involvement of others, and their own unpredictable decision making, and the sustenance that needs to be received so the manifestation begins to take place, we can never be 100% sure, nor guarantee perfect results infallibly.

SCRIPTURAL REF. HOSEA CHAPTERS 1, 2 AND 3

[1]The word of the Lord that came unto Hosea, the son of Beeir, in the days of Uzziah, Jotham, Ahaz, and Hezekiah, kings of Judah, and in the days of Jeroboam the son of Joash, king of Israel.[2]The beginning of the word of the Lord by Hosea. And the Lord said to Hosea, Go, take unto thee a wife of whoredoms and children of whoredoms: for the land hath committed great whoredom, departing from the Lord.[3]So he went and took Gomer the daughter of Diblaim; which conceived, and bare him a son.[4]And the Lord said unto him, Call his name Jezreel; for yet a little while and I will avenge the blood of Jezreel upon the house of Jehu, and will cause to cease the kingdom of the house of Israel.[5]And it shall come to pass at that day, that I will break the bow of Israel in the valley of Jezreel.[6]And she conceived again and bare a daughter. And God said unto him, Call her name Lo-ruhamah: for I will no more have mercy upon the house of Israel; but I will utterly take them away.[7]But I will have mercy upon

the house of Judah, and will save them by the Lord their God, and not save them by bow, nor by sword, nor by battle, by horses, nor by horsemen. [8]Now when she had weaned Lo-ruhamah, she conceived, and bare a son. [9]Then said God, Call his name Lo-anni: for ye are not my people, and I will not be your God. [10]Yet the number of the children of Israel shall be as the sand of the sea, which cannot be measured nor numbered; and it shall come to pass, that in the place where it was said unto them, Ye are not my people, there it shall be said unto them, Ye are the sons of the living God. [11]Then shall the children of Judah and the children of Israel be gathered together, and appointed themselves one head, and they shall come up out of the land: for great shall be the day of Jezreel.

CHAPTER 2

[1]Say ye unto your brethren, Ammi; and to your sisters, Ruhamah. [2]Plead with your mother, plead: for she is not my wife, neither am I her husband: let her therefore put away her whoredoms out of sight, and her adulteries from between her breasts; [3]Lest I strip her naked, and set her as in the day that she was born, and make her as a wilderness, and set her like a dry land, and slay her with thirst. [4]And I will not have mercy upon her children; for they be the children of whoredoms. [5]For their mother hath played the harlot: she that conceived them hath done shamefully: for she said, I will go after my lovers, that give me my bread and my water, my wool and my flax, mine oil and my drink. [6]Therefore behold, I will hedge up thy way with thorns, and make a wall, that she shall not find her path. [7]And she shall follow after her lovers, but she shall

not overtake them; and she shall seek them, but shall not find them: then shall she say, I will go and return to my first husband: for then was it better with me than now. [8]For she did not know that I gave her corn, and wine, and oil, and multiplied her silver and gold, which they prepared for Baal. [9]Therefore will I return, and take away my corn in the time thereof, and my wine in the season thereof, and will recover my wool and my flax given to cover her nakedness. [10]And now will I discover her lewdness in the sight of her lovers, and none shall deliver her out of mine hand. I will also cause all her mirth to cease, *her feast days,* her new moons, and her Sabbaths, and all her *solemn feasts.* [12] And I will destroy her vines and her fig trees, whereof she hath said, These are my rewards that my lovers have given me: and I will make them a forest, and the beasts of the field shall eat them. [13]And I will visit upon her the days of Baalim, wherein she burnt incense to them, and she decked herself with her earrings and her jewels, and she went after her lovers, and forgat me, saith the Lord. [14]Therefore behold, I will allure her, and bring her into the wilderness, and speak comfortably unto her. [15]And I will give her her vineyards from thence, and the valley of Achor for a door of hope: and she shall sing there, as in the days of her youth, and as in the day when she came up out of the land of Egypt. [16]And it shall be at that day, saith the Lord, that thou shalt call me Ishi: and shalt call me no more Baali. [17]For I will take away the names of Baalim out of her mouth, and they shall no more be remembered by their name. [18]And in that day will I make a covenant for them with the beasts of the field, and with the fowls of heaven, and with the creeping things of the ground: and I will break the bow and the sword and the battle out of the earth and will make them to lie down safely. [19]And I will betroth thee unto me forever, yea, I will betroth thee unto me in righteousness, and in judgment, and in loving kindness, and in mercies. [20]I will even betroth thee unto me in faithfulness: and thou shalt know the Lord. [21]And it shall come to pass in that day, I will hear, saith the Lord, I will hear the heavens, and they shall hear the earth; [22]And the earth shall hear the corn, and the wine, and the oil; and they shall hear Jezreel. [23]And I will sow her unto me in the earth; and I will have mercy upon her that had not obtained mercy; and I will say to them which were not my people, Thou art my people; and they shall say, Thou art my God.

CHAPTER 3

[1]Then said the Lord unto me, Go yet, love a woman beloved of her friend, yet an adulteress, according to the love of the Lord toward the children of Israel, who look to other gods, and love flagons of wine. [2]So I bought her to me for fifteen pieces of silver, and for a homer of barley, and a half homer of barley: [3]And I said unto her, Thou shalt abide for me many days; thou shalt not play the harlot, and thou shalt not be for another man: so will I also be for thee. [4]For the children of Israel shall abide many days without a king, and without a prince, and without a sacrifice, and without an image, and without an ephod, and without teraphim: [5]Afterward shall the children of Israel return, and seek the Lord their God, and David their king; and shall fear the Lord and his goodness in the latter days.

What Do You Know? Is It Real?

SCRIPTURAL REF. HOLY QURAN 18:60-82

⁶⁰And when Moses said to his servant: I will not cease until I reach the junction of the two rivers, otherwise I will go on for years. ⁶¹So when they reached the junction of the two (rivers), they forgot their fish, and it took its way into the river, being free. ⁶²But when they had gone further, he said to this servant: Bring to us our morning meal, certainly we have found fatigue in this our journey. ⁶³He said: Sawest thou when we took refuge on the rock, I forgot the fish, and none but the devil made me forget to speak of it, and it took its way into the river; what a wonder. ⁶⁴He said: This is what we sought for. So they returned retracing their footsteps. ⁶⁵Then they found one of Our servants whom We had granted mercy from Us and whom We had taught knowledge from Ourselves. ⁶⁶Moses said to him: May I follow thee that thou mayest teach me of the good thou has been taught? ⁶⁷He said: Thou canst not have patience with me.⁶⁸And how canst thou have patience in that whereof thou hast not a comprehensive knowledge? ⁶⁹He said: If Allah please, thou wilt find me patient, nor shall I disobey thee in aught. ⁷⁰He said: If thou wouldst follow me, question me not about aught until I myself speak to thee about it.⁷¹So they set out until, when they embarked in a boat, he made a hole in it. (Moses) said: Hast thou made a hole in it to drown its occupants? Thou hast surely done a grievous thing. ⁷²He said: Did I not say that thou couldst not have patience with me? ⁷³He said: Blame me not for what I forgot and be not hard upon me for what I did. ⁷⁴So they went on, until when they met a boy, he slew him. (Moses) said: Hast thou slain an

innocent person, not guilty of slaying another? Thou hast indeed done a horrible thing. [75]He said: Did I not say to thee that thou couldst not have patience with me? [76]He said: If I ask thee about anything after this, keep not company with me. Thou wilt then indeed have found an excuse in my case. [77]So they went on, until when they came to the people of a town, they asked its people for food, but they refused to entertain them as guest. Then they found in it a wall which was on the point of falling, so he put it into a right state. (Moses) said: If thou hadst wished, thou couldst have taken a recompense for it. [78]He said: This is the parting between me and thee. Now I will inform thee of the significance of that with which thou couldst not have patience. [79]As for the boat, it belonged to poor people working on the river, and I intended to damage it, for there was behind them a king who seized every boat by force. [80]And as for the boy, his parents were believers and we feared lest he should involve them in wrongdoing and disbelief. [81]So we intended that their Lord might give them in his place one better in purity and nearer to mercy. [82]And as for the wall, it belonged to two orphan boys in the city, and there was beneath it a treasure belonging to them, and their father had been a righteous man. So thy Lord intended that they should attain their maturity and take out their treasure- a mercy from thy Lord and I did not do it of my own accord. This is the significance of that with which thou couldst not have patience.

The initial lesson is to recognize something. That something might have been a dream, an experience, a circumstance or anything that the mind has previously perceived without our full awareness. It is the point where one must be willing, because he is now able, to create a change in himself.

These two narratives from these two Holy books aren't only comparable because they are part of the Abrahamic Lineage of religious script. They are comparable because they first begin with the teacher being taught, the instructor being instructed, as to what it is that's in him that he needs to not only see in the people, but to also be able to have compassion and empathy to deal with, and correct them, because of his own experience. That should be this "Revel"

To recognize an experience, and its meaning is one of the most profound things one can do. To draw out any and every lesson, comprehend how it defines Life's moments, and then reveal it to one and all is the full purpose of our experiences. They aren't just moments of good or bad feelings, what is going on in our lives are the results of decisions that stretch as far back as our youth.

Those decisions, and all of those leading up to now, have to be, need to be, re-evaluated, comprehended, and learned from so that a fuller meaning of present life is grasped. We do not have a full meaning of anything if this process isn't carried out. What we think we know is only a partial, minute, part of everything that's going on with us. Knowing just a little of what really was going on in our past decisions can expand our knowledge beyond our present imagination's reach. It's not just the memories that we remember that are relevant. Most of the things we experience in our lives are from decisions and memories that we have lost all recollection to their existence.

So what is it about fate that makes it our scapegoat? Most of those who believe in destiny discount the fact that destiny is not a spontaneous event, but an actual calculation. There is no sensible way to come to a result without first having a calculation, to some degree, done. Many forget this and give destiny, or fate, a bad reputation for showing up at the wrong, or inappropriate time. But we never ask ourselves what is it that we really should want? Well, if we don't answer this question sufficiently then destiny or fate will show up, but it won't be inappropriate or wrong, your thought of it will be. Making no decision is making a decision for the wrong or inappropriate thing to show up.

Our elders, holy men, prophets, teachers, messengers, and messiahs do not just happen to be the way that they are revealed to us. It takes a process of inner realization and inner knowledge to bring them up to the point where we usually find them. This Revelation in Duty is done through the process of purging what's in them that can, and will, hinder their individual growth and enlightenment; so that they are familiar with the state and condition that the people themselves are similarly in. One who raises his people comes from among them so that this recognition can be made.

What we have in our two narratives are the growth processes that was needed in order to reveal a misconception that could then be the trigger for elevation. Our elders were able to build on their new perspectives and new overstandings, of themselves. Because, in all of life, nothing can be done without an experience attached to it. That's not how the brain and its creating works. The brain will put two things together, that have nothing to do with one another, just so that it can have its conclusion. So nothing is as simple as meaning one thing. The deeper we go, or the higher we go, we find more than we have ever thought about before.

So why do we have these experiences that are part of a purging process leading to growth and enlightenment? Because, without them our knowledge becomes arrogance instead of wisdom. We will feel privileged like all is already ours or given to us, feeling chosen but not acting the part.

You see purging, and its process, allows us to revisit that stuff that is buried under our new founded identity; that we think is sturdy and stable. But to Our surprise, what's buried is unstable, toxic, and volatile. So if it is not removed, it will eventually, raise its ugly head up, or its several heads, and ruin that newly created structure. All because it wants the state and condition of things to remain the same. It doesn't like change, doesn't want change, doesn't want anything to do with change because it was non-change that made it that ugly beast that it is. That's why we need the assistance of an experience that causes one to take action of a different type. We sometimes need the extreme situations of Hosea to wake us up to our duty, or the disappointment of Moses to get us to move forward with that chip on our shoulders; ready to prove the world wrong. In the case of Moses, even though the wise man revealed certain truths, it was the experience that he was to take the most from. It was the negative thoughts, the pride in voicing his opinion, the arrogance of judgment he cast at the wise man that he was supposed to recognize as areas of concern and correction in himself. We must do the same. That is why we must identify with the highest character we can imagine. Only identifying with the Ultimate Principle will create an environment of constant change, or rather progress, towards pure knowledge and wisdom. If we continue to only identify ourselves with being mankind, then we will constantly fail, and suffer, in gaining anything righteous.

    The two narratives give us the full spectrum of the constant attention that's needed to continue on a path of a higher character. Hosea's narrative allows us to consider a practical way that we can refine ourselves and purge away any impurities. The compassion needed for that type of wife, the understanding that one must have, builds very strong resilience in a man. The empathy that is shared towards her creates a remarkable teacher, leader, and righteous one. Courage is then seen in more ways than just bodily. One loses nothing but gains everything.

Nature is Neuter, so is the divine neutral. Divinity is neither bad nor good, it's neither right or wrong. What it is, is applicable to the growth, development, and betterment of an individual, and people. Nothing is ever a waste, everything is expendable. Einstein revealed to us $E=MC^2$ (E= MC squared) for this very reason. It teaches us that everything does transform from one state to another, keeping life in a balanced or neutral state, comparable to Ultimate Reality.

Will . . . what a very powerful attribute to ponder and conceptualize. The will is what's needed when one seeks to change or transform any entity from one state to another. But one needs to learn about his own will and how it works. The ways that attempt to explain or define the Will are as many as there are those who consider it. No two ways fully duplicate each other in the description of what the will is, and how it works. But there needs to be some understanding of this as it applies to any and every subject, because, without it, no strides can be made. What I mean is that there is either a portion of will applied to any and every thought or act performed, or there is a lack of a portion of will applied to any and every thought or act performed. Our problem is that we don't know, in either case, should we apply more or less. So the will goes unchecked and does more harm than good. Knowing Thyself will assist anyone in this area of underdevelopment.

When are we going to reach the junction of our journey where we create Life Changing Impulses? We are all life traveling without the slightest idea as to the totality of our journey. Yes, some know about a few ideals, and others got a few concepts on deck, but who knows the total destination, the grand design, our full-length feature? And who would overstand such an elaborate Revelation? That's why it takes the work and words of many to set us straight. But we don't listen, or when that teacher moves on we change things, or we put up half the effort.

The influx of ideals or ideas in traditions is where straying from the Truth of Revelation, or of that in which we originally believed in, begins. There is a system of inception that most of us are not fully aware of, and this system is our greatest adversary. Why is that? Well, it is because the human being, and the human body, are designed to receive so much more than it is designed to transmit or give. Now at the subconscious level, the mind is equal in the receiving and transmitting ability. But at the conscious level, the ability of sense perception overwhelms us. So much so till we begin to accept pleasure even in pain, and it becomes our daily bread. This is what leads us to concretize our lives into traditions. The Conservative Concretizing of Traditions will definitely cause a man, and a people, to stray by stagnation and forget their Revelation in Duty. The mere fact of life is that everything is moving. That movement is in the form of a

Vibration that cannot be turned off. It is this reason that is at the root of progress.

Our progress through life is totally dependent on us not becoming concretized in traditions. In order to get from Point A to Point B we must be willing to follow our heart and mind, stimulated by an ideal that has comprehensible ideas, for our necessity. How else, or in what other way, do we actually move? There is none. There is no other way that a man moves but by the way he comprehends or feels about a particular thing. If we are to ever get to that junction, that changes our lives and leads us onward, we had better be able to recognize it, or else we will, most certainly, plow right by it by being concretized in traditions.

———◆———

Some of us are practitioners, and we advance when necessary, reproving truths to contemporary standards are reveling in duty. Others are traditionalist, who disastrously remain the same, they have indurated their faith and belief, that originally brought about a change, into a final state of repetition and stagnation.

So how do we know who is who or what is what? Well, the key is practicality. If what we believe in can't be used daily, then it is of no good to us. We need to start realizing that God is concerned with our everyday issues, and not just some religious stuff we attend too. Who put religion in a corner of the week? Who said that there are only certain times and certain places that we are supposed to worship, believe, have faith in, and call on God? Don't be an idiot, God cannot be regulated to any idea of man's. He is the One Who Regulates, He Sets the Standards, not us, and His Standards are set up upon the Eternal and Infinite. We just need to identify them, and then live by them, as they are, Truthfully!

A Competitive nature is one of the stages of development of a male. How can he find his place without striving for it against any trial or tribulation that is pitted against him, including his fellow man? He does this as he develops his mental and physical bodies. And continues mentally when the physical reaches its peak. This is Revelation in Duty.

It's the identification of the rate, in striving through our subjective conceptualization, that gives us a location of our progress of our higher selves. The subjective concept is itself a high form of thought and thinking. It is the beginning of dissecting our objective world into a more meaningful reality. We do not need the object, which itself perishes. What needs to be gained is the subject that began the object's manifestation. It's a return to the origin, which allows everyone to have a journey, a path, a way to start living in their own Revelation.

Our subjective observation has been replaced with psychological evaluation which limits the expression down to explanation, unsuited for the goals achieved by our ancestors. Less is more, more is less. We have to turn about our direction into every aspect searched out. The completed has to become undone, the unfinished is what needs to be completed. Opening, waking, rising, doing, knowing, these are our classes, or levels, our degrees of certification in Revelation. It is a subjective fact that all things, even a lie is founded, and dependent, on the Truth, which is the origin, otherwise none of it, nothing, can exist. You can Disagree but prove that this is wrong for greater development and higher elevation.

How is it that in every physical way one can be a militant, a soldier, but not in intellect, knowledge, or wisdom? Who feels not like a soldier in their subjective warfare against BABYLON? Its attack, its infiltration, its captivity is beyond the physical, so one must defend from beyond the physical. We must have Revelation in Duty

We were people who planned for tomorrow, observed the distant future, but now we only look at today. Which has caused a limitation, created a blur between what's real and what isn't real. Real is that which never passes away. What isn't real is that which does. So where do you think our collective focus lies? Yeah, there are a few of us on it, but that isn't enough to do all of us any good. We all must contribute, knowingly, to this cause. What are we afraid of? We cannot afford this fear, this terror of accomplishing greatness. Embrace what's strange, take on the different. It is in this liberty that freedom is gained.

The two types that we are dealing with are those who don't have enough time to gain the serious dedication and devotion that is necessary for growth and servantship, and one who lacks the experience that would stimulate and motivate a drive towards growth and servantship. Both suffer from a form of immaturity in subjective conceptualization that hinders the progress of our people, and humanity. They are the ones who forget our Revelations.

As our body, and mind, fight against the bombardment of so many forces unknown to our focal consciousness, what is it that we should be doing to assist in this combat situation? This question is the single most important question we can ask ourselves at any point in our lives. It's a question of direction, a question of evaluation, a question of survey, and a question of correction.

When our future weighs more than our past we neglect to question anything other than pleasure and desire. But once our past begins to amass the weight of our future, pleasure and desire must be replaced with fate and destiny, or many other far mind grasping concepts that stimulate thought and thinking beyond the self. If we really listen to the flesh it will ask for things different than our overstanding has given us. We lack in the comprehension of the flesh, and so we misdiagnose or misread its needs, giving rise to a third party who is not a natural manifestation of our own ability, but an unnatural manifestation of our inability.

With better awareness some of us will become true practitioners of life, and advance when able or necessary. Others will stay blind, weak and terrified traditionalist, who fatally remain the same. How is it that we cannot see that we each create, in our own ways? By design, creation is as infinite as time and needs all of our assistance in its Revelations.

Between the two fields that we are involved in, the collective Magnetic of the earth and the individual Morphic, we must begin to recognize our connection, and further our interdependence upon each other. The subject of Moses, in the Quran, isn't a necessary connection with Hosea simply because Moses is a forefather of Hosea, and that that preceding is also pointed out in the bible. The subject of Moses, as expressed in the Quran, points to the connectivity of both of the Holy Books. They express a completeness that wouldn't be seen in just one or the other. In grammatical terms its subject and predicate, noun and verb, a beginning and conclusion. While both are of the Abrahamic lineage, and in general would be how we see them in our Magnetic Field Perception, and recognize them as beneficial in one aspect or another, it is the balance that one creates between the two, in his own Morphic Field Perception, that gives us the highest benevolence. Using both Holy books in their clear perspective will reveal much for us to revel in. The Coalescing that is discovered in such study is a True Revelation in Duty.

3

Inference is Movement

    Inference is a reaching of one step after another has been made certain and is true to its purpose. The key is knowing its purpose. Without knowing the purpose of the preceding step another step cannot be taken. Inference is the process we use to make that step certain. Inferring allows the coming forth of a resolution in the thinking or pondering of a message, and messenger. Inference is the building of the connections of truths heretofore unknown or unrecognized.

    All of Life share a commonality in origin, and in the way of advancement. It is our different rates of advancement that gives the appearance of difference in origin. Our societies are not separate, individual entities. If we were to look at them from an elevated position of observance, we would see how each aspect is an inference of some aspect of another, seemingly different, society.

Think of the ancient people of Babel and how they built in one tongue and with one mind. Even though a confounding of the tongues was laid upon them the contextual meanings were still present. Their ideas of living were the same as they were before, they just didn't have the immediate ability to share them. If the different tongues are attributed to being born at this moment, then so also was inference. At that moment, in a different way of speech, they still lived according to the way they had previously been taught, just in a changed way of sharing and expressing it. That inference is still being reflected today.

Inference is a unifying principle. It is in the area of coalescing qualities that it has to be re-introduced and clearly defined; with a positive purpose in use. We have gone past a positive use for our tools and now only seek the negativity that they reveal. We have become very pessimistic in our outlook of things, which has led us to these gloomy times. Our defining and use of inference here seeks to change this perspective. The belief in God itself is a conclusion of the process of inferring, which is inference. The Divine is an inference that is made when a paramount is reached in the totality of that which we become aware of. There is never an observable physical connection, but our inference might as well be called one because of its actuality. So in this instance, we are defining inference from the Benevolence of The Divine.

BIBLE REF. KJV MALACHI 3:1; ISAIAH 45:7; ECCLESIASTES 12:13-14

Malachi 3:1

Behold I will send my messenger, and he shall prepare a way before me: and the Lord, whom ye seek, shall suddenly come to his temple, even the messenger of the covenant, whom ye delight in: behold, he shall come, saith the Lord of host.

Isaiah 45:7

I form the light, and create darkness: I make peace, and create evil: I the Lord do all these things.

Ecclesiastes 12:13-14

Let us hear the conclusion of the whole matter: Fear God, and keep his commandments: for this is the whole duty of man. [14]For God shall bring every work into judgment, with every secret thing, whether it be good, or whether it be evil.

HOLY QURAN REF. 2:25; 7:7; 57:4

Ch. 2 The Cow 2:25

And give good news to those who believe and do good deeds, that for them are Gardens in which rivers flow. Whenever they are given a portion of the fruit thereof, they will say: This is what was given to us before; and they are given the like of it. And for them therein are pure companions and therein they will abide.

Ch. 7: The Elevated places 7:7

Then surely We shall relate to them with knowledge and We are never absent.

Ch. 57 Iron 57:4

It is He who created the heavens and earth in six periods, and He is established on the Throne of power. He knows that which goes down into the earth and that which come forth out of it, and that which comes down from Heaven and that which goes up to it. And He is with you wherever you are. And Allah is seer of what you do.

Inference is the advance place of reasoning and overstanding. If we are to come from any place or go to any state it is inference that will get us there. Inferring is the tying of the knot or the loosening of one. It helps one consider other probabilities and possibilities. There is nothing that is, or can be done, or known, that is absolutely independent of everything else, making inference a foundation of Life.

Inference is reached when one passes from one or more propositions, statements, or judgments, considered as true, to another truth of which is believed to follow that of the former.

Now based on that definition, inference has within its process a pattern. This pattern is that which either allows or disallows what is being inferred. It is another system within proving that even inference itself isn't independent. Inference can even be defined as a pattern in a general sense, because all that is inferred agrees with the other qualities of the origin, in a continuous stream.

But what is it about a pattern that could lend itself to us in overstanding the complexity of an inference. Let's break down what I mean by a pattern. First off, Patterns speak to us. What they say depends on our perception. If and when we notice a pattern it is stating something that should otherwise be obvious. We fight against the knowledge of patterns and what they say, and most are too stubborn-minded to perceive and know that. But a pattern is just like any other organism. It is built from the constituents of all of its parts and systems. Therefore, it removes all doubt as to the accidental or coincidental aspects that could be associated with it. Looking keenly, one cannot misjudge a pattern. Where it comes from, or begin, and the results of it are as concrete as any proven principle in physics. Where we are failing is in realizing its meaning.

Usually, the results of an unrecognizable pattern are not seen simply because they are not in agreement with what our focal consciousness has decided that it wants for itself. There is some form of pleasure or benefit in it, that is clouding the better judgment that should be there. Now what we have to accept is that it's a pattern for a reason, and that reason is because a decision has to be made in order to alter or change the results, that are soon to arrive, to a more truthful and beneficial one towards our goal. A pattern is telling us that we cannot accomplish a higher good choosing and accepting this certain way. It is screaming for change.

Now this is where inference steps in. All bodies of information have contextual results of them that are based on the pattern of the components working together. Once this is realized an inference can be made and the steps retaken, with the new input, to produce a different outcome. It is why the different messengers do speak of the same source, but to a type and kind that's all their own. We are all conspiring in our inferences.

Take the Holy Scripts for an example, they all have a source of Divinity that is beyond this world, but yet is the Creator of it, and yet, is a part of it. The appearance of difference is where inference is allowed to create the environment necessary for the attainment of the Awareness of the Divinity. And just because an inference may be artfully decorated, by the environment that it is in, doesn't mean that it is different from another environment that's seeking similar attainment. Inference allows for variations so long as they remain true to the source.

Inference is also a feeling inside. It is a feeling in the depth of one's self that announces a truth to him. This is how one remains true to the source. He has to feel it, and then he will know it. There is nothing better equipped to show us a truth than to feel it. Being in this manifested world has numbed us to these internal feelings that guide us. To the point where they are difficult to even recognize. Receptivity to our deep feelings is weakened by this world and its sense stimuli. It is why we must become aware of this way of notification, through practice, and adjust to its unveiling that leads to comprehension.

The feeling that inference establishes is malleable. This malleability is the process of inferring that either further establishes the current conclusion or produces another inference from a premise still being reasoned. While some current state may hold the attention at present, the source is never abandoned nor forgotten, it is always relative in the process regulating truth in portions throughout the inferring.

Inference has the ability to bring two seemingly unlike things together by finding the common thread between them, like apples and oranges both being fruits. The common thread of things is often deeply kept truths that one must search out and earn for revelation. Just as the key unlocks the tumbler, and the tumbler unlocks the lock, we need to take a more intrinsic look at everything to gather its true identity, therefore rendering facts and truths towards our inference.

All things have a relationship with all other things, even if that relationship is only one's relativity to the other. That relativity, being the common thread, can be inferred upon as a relationship between them. This is the realm of inference. This is the location of truths that lend us their assistance for as long as we ask. Knowledge is gained here, clarity, shifts in perspectives, understanding, and wisdom. We begin to operate at potential when we are making inferences.

Whether religious, with the belief in God or an agnostic, with the belief that God nor any ultimate reality can be known, even if it does exist, the function that transports one through towards any conclusion, is his inference of the facts that can attest to his subject.

The scriptures are for the former, and in this case, that's who is being addressed. We are addressing he who believes in God and is giving him a tool to deepen that belief with the assistance of the Holy Bible and Holy Quran. But this isn't a skill to simply address one aspect of an individual's perspective of life. Meaning, this and all other skills and abilities of mental, cognitive, and subjective thinking are for tangible and intangible realms. Where we exist and operate in one should be reflected as identical in another and does. There is no faking in this, our perception is our reality, and our reality is our apprehension of what we have concluded in our inference of *perception*. Where we are weak, subjectively, we will infer that objectively, and where we are strong subjectively we will infer that. In other words, the subjective is the essence of a thing, and if one cannot grasp the essential he will be easily persuaded, in the physical, to do the opposite in our manifested world. But if one is strong in inferring, he will be able to produce strong-minded views of things that essentially exist beyond his mind.

Inference is a magical balancing act of the mind. It is something the mind actually wants to do, just on a deeper level. You see, the mind, through the brain, is constantly making sense of the things it receives through the senses;

by creating relationships with other things it already possesses. For example, a desk, table, bench and counter top all share a relationship in the mind of being able to support things on their surfaces. No one consciously does this. The mind is designed to make our worlds make sense, and so we have an untapped ability that can service our entire lives better; rather than just being one of our automated systems that we pay little attention to. The mind uses this system to unite the entire universe, so why not benefit from this ability by becoming conscious of it, and realize the unifiable possibilities starting with the coalescing of our Sacred Scripts? It is simply building a relationship between Truths, Truths that happen to be relative anyway.

At the least, our inferences should be of a reckoning nature. As divided as the world is, every unifying mechanism needs to be known and utilized for the greater good of all people. The times of agreeing to disagree are over. How is it possible to live in the same world and not have the views that possess similarities? That means that our focus is elsewhere and not in Living.

When we make inferences, some are as clear as any mundane thing in our daily lives, but at other times, our inferences might as well be earth and water because their relationship may be as deep as the age of the universe. But that's no reason or excuse to justify a non-relative conclusion. All things have in them a true commonality that can be inferred upon to bring about a better understanding of this life and the world it's lived in.

What inference can we make out of Malachi 3:1 and Surah 7:7? A messenger must have a message, and that message should be one that's full of knowledge that benefits the messenger and those to whom the message is delivered. A simple and clear inference is made that says that we should be on the lookout for such a one, and that he will teach us great teachings that are beyond our own abilities to know right off, but that an explanation will make the knowledge knowable.

Another inference can be made from the verse that speaks of a way being prepared, and that whom we seek will suddenly come to his temple and, in Surah 7: 7, that "we are never absent". The inference of the availability of assistance from on high can be truly inferred from these segments of the Sacred Scripts. For we can infer that God, in whatever form necessary, is here guiding us on and always present. And lastly, Malachi speaks of being in delight, while Surah 7: 7 says that we shall relate to them. Both of these convey the inference of following. Whether in delight, or in relating, there has to be a "following of" in order to achieve either of these. So following the messenger and his message is the greatest inference that can be made.

In Isaiah 45:7 it begins with the form of light and darkness being created, while Surah 57:4 begins with the heavens and earth being created in six periods. The inference here is that out of God all things do appear to take positions, depending on their design. Nothing can appear out of place because it is the Most High who orders it. Peace and evil are comparable to heaven and earth, for there is no evil in heaven and no peace on earth. This inference tells us what we can expect and prepare for as we journey through life. These scriptures wrap up with a confirmation of God's power, presence, and knowing of all things that are here with us, even the secret things.

Ecclesiastes 12:13-14 and Surah 2:25 gives us the inference of righteous. If anyone decided to define righteousness it would not be complete without the descriptions given from these two scripts. We know what is expected of us, where we are to look for instruction, and if there's reward or benefit, or consequence. We can rely on doing good, and being good, to produce positive results in our lives, and know what our deeds are being measured up against. Our work, that which we wrought with our own hands, our actions, and our labors, will all be given the scrutiny in judgment and reveal the truth that it conceals.

4

Self-Seeking Self, Seeking Self

In defining Self, we must use the scripts, terms, texts, and narratives, that are applicable, from many schools of thought, that are able to explain what we wish to convey to you concerning what it is that is in each of us, and that is all of us.

We believe that there is so much more to man than flesh and bones, and more than the average mind realizes. Therefore, an expansive library of information and knowledge is needed to define him, and that is how we will partially define Self.

The Self is Everything, All Things, No Thing, The Only Thing. The different degrees, levels, and categories create the truth of all these designations. The Self is manifold and plenteous in substance and content. We assert that any attempt at the full description or definition of Self will require the assistance of the sciences, doctrines, and philosophies of the entire world. Making separation a blindness, but coaction and coadaptation venerably wise.

SCRIPTURAL REF. HOLY QURAN & HOLY BIBLE

In the Holy Quran, where Bashar, Ins, Insan, Insiy, Rajul, Nas (self) is mentioned. We have 79 suras and 421 ayats.

In the Holy Bible where we have man or mankind (self) is mentioned we have 60 Books and 2,603 verses.

It is said that one must "Know Thy Self" in this world. What that means, in part, is that we must know what is going on with ourselves at all times. Whether that's tangible or intangible, it doesn't matter. We must be fully aware, focally conscious, of everything that either affects us or that we affect. By the Self being ethereal its able to extend into any application of our lives. It has no limits, and has within it the ability of entanglement. As a matter of fact, the Self's Entanglement is multi-capable. It can literally be in many places at once. If it was ever possible to know something so powerful, so vast, but yet immediate, and that life itself is seen, seemingly, with another's perspective, it is the knowledge of Self.

As we exist today, the knowledge of Self is foreign. We literally don't know who or what we are, even though we do know that we are. We are Self-aware, but not Self-knowledgeable. And to make matters more complicated, the Self doesn't even fit into any particular category. I mean . . . is it psychological, religious, or social?

What Do You Know? Is It Real?

The Self has many descriptions, definitions, and theories given to us since ancient times. One would think that a conceptual subject like Self would be readily perceptible to us by now. But even with all of the commentaries, speeches, knowledge and information available, we still seem to have a truncated understanding of Self. The beneficial correctitude seems to be lost, either in translation or explanation, of this ancient subject of contemplation.

The Self is so expansive that narrowing down a definitive description of the Self is equivalent to describing who and what God Himself is. Reason being is that our experiences have a lot to say about this particular subjective subject. And based on Relativity, all of us have divergent experiences, of our particular objectivity, from one another. In other words, we don't all see the same thing at the same time, which creates variations between us. These variations can be slight or extreme. From a single circumstance, one can perceive innocuously while the other perceives perniciously.

Have you ever wondered what it would feel like to be exactly as you should be? To say and do exactly what was meant for you, and to only allow what's good for you to exist? What if I told you that you are already using what would create all that for you? If you have thought about this at least once in your life, then good for you. Now stop thinking this way and start being this way. If you have not ever thought in this way, then I got to ask you, "What have you been thinking about, who are you, and what are you doing here?"

I'm asking this question to the perfect you, your Self. I'm not asking the you who you think you are right now. The you right now is not a very nice person, whether you realize it or not. Living in this world is not conducive to the highest moral character traits or untainted intellect. In this world we are all engineered with a devilish and demonic mindset, capable of the best, but, more often than not, manifesting our worse. So being who you want to be now, in your current state, may not be your true best. To be who yourself is, requires knowledge of the best potential you. A justifiable you from the depth of your own innocent self. A you that is indifferent to poverty or wealth.

You have to begin by imagining Self and its ways which would probably be 180° different from you and your ways. How, do you ask, is it that you've become so unfamiliar to your own Self? Well, we've all become unfamiliar with our own Self simply because we are a living organism. Being a living organism means that we are constantly reproducing ourselves. Now molecularly that is all fine and well, but when we reproduce on a level above that, like psychologically, we start to loose ourselves down dark unknown paths and become lost. These paths are the sense stimuli that we turn our attention to. Things that satisfy our bodies but not necessarily our Mind or Self. Foods, intoxicants, sex, entertainment, and a myriad of other things all create a pathway away from Self. With that happening we become lost as to our true fundamental identity. This reproducing is natural on a molecular scale, but can have detrimental results on our Larger System. This is an automated function that can create disastrous consequences if left unattended.

We become physical beings through conception, but there is Great Evidence that shows, and proves, that there is more to us; like the voice that we hear in our minds, that have no lips or vocal cords, but we can hear it. Our intuitive identity is a form of that evidence. Our Déjá Vu moments are proofs without a doubt. Our essence is not the current state of our focal consciousness, but is a very high level, continuous, energetic state seated within our minds, which could be eons in age, and whose origin is incomprehensible to us.

Our purpose then is to continue to gather the experiences of decisions and information that should lead to an expected, and capable of being known, Self. The Self is the reason behind all and everything. It gives us purpose, and that is powerful enough to know it, not just know of it.

That brings us to our successes and failures in life. Do they really carry the value that our scrutiny gives them? Is there reason for the condemnation of what appears to be done wrong, or the praise of what appears to have been done right? We have to consider that the value in the experience of both is a gain, if we can comprehend it as such. Without this comprehension, of what we evaluate life to be, experience, we fall short and become superficial and not purposeful towards the Self.

Either in actuality, discussion, or a meditative experience, the imprint of life's circumstances, on the mind, for study, must be gained so that the knowledge of the experience becomes beneficial results. We are struggling because we are not satisfying the complete spectrum of our existence.

Sustained effort towards Self, and avoiding frivolous distractions, set us on a course of Great Success. With diverse perception, we can recognize all of the changes that come to manifest in our lives, and keep that which is good, while crucifying that which isn't. Our awareness of proclivitical physical weaponry will increase our sensitivity to, and defense against, subtle attacks. The one thing that we must really understand is that there is no one absolute, fail proof, fool proof, guaranteed way to get this done. We have to engage in the teachings of multiple disciplines of self-improvement, religion and education. Every system has their individual mastery of a defense for an improvement of Self. And while I hate to be a bearer of bad news, I have to confess that it is every man, or woman, for themselves. We are assisted by our leaders, teachers, guides; and our gurus, messiahs, messengers and prophets, nevertheless, it is up to each and every one of us, individually, then collectively, to recognize the skills and abilities needed, and then acquire them towards the achievement of Self-knowledge.

Each of us has to design our own system to accomplish the self-awareness that's full of self-knowledge. This system can be tweaked and attached to an already existing system, a combination of more than one system, or a totally new design with only a semblance of any of the previous systems. Some of us may have to be more creative than others since self-knowledge requires modification within specific experiences, but modified towards its truth.

Learning relative truths in concise steps towards Our Essence will elevate us in our experiences. Our environments, communities, and nations are filled with all of the necessities of life, including failures and successes. We constantly struggle with all of the so-called rights and wrongs as if one, at the expense of the other, will ultimately do us any good. Polarities are the components of decision making, not a way to live. We are not designed to live in extreme circumstances. We are temperate beings because the Self must be balanced. That's why even slight changes affect us. So balance is our quintessential state to achieve while physical. This will lead to that comprehension of Self. Understand that there is a time for all things. To accomplish this balance, we must find, focus and follow the Silver Cord that runs through the cultures, civilizations, religions, philosophies and laws of the entire world.

Development of the subtle intellect would be a great ability for all. If one desires a certain state, then he has to accept the teachings and disciplines that help him achieve this state. This can be recognized immediately for a select few, but usually requires years of effort on one's part. You have to be the type who is not such a traditionalist for chronological order of a study. Because I'm telling you that this Self comes to you in parts, sections, and arrangements from every possible direction, dimension, and degree. It's spread out everywhere, and we have to look, research, find and learn of it from everywhere.

When it comes to the knowledge of Self we cannot continue to allow empyreal wisdom, in its vastness, to be the product of a few empirics who create doctrines that they themselves cannot follow. If so, we shall continue to suffer, and we will never know Self. At any given time, there are aspects of the empyreal that are revealed, and others that are enshrouded from being known in that particular way. It is why our studies must be diverse. The partiality that enshroudment causes creates the opportunity for diversity. This is the mystery of wisdom and its guidance. We are being directed to diversity. We just refuse to acknowledge it by thinking that we could become bad Jew, Christian, Muslim, Hebrew, Hindu, Buddhist or others. We need it all to know Self, because no one and nothing is wrong, it's all relative.

I know what you're thinking, if it's all relative then why can't just one work to know the Self? Well, it's because the Self is Absolute, and the Absolute is Measureless. Now in this immeasurability is the Absolute's ability to appropriate to itself a measure for our comprehension, but, we really start out as only Self, and is absolute in that. We don't necessarily go to that. What we actually do is remember and comprehend creations inter-connectedness and its interdependence as a singularity even with its diversity and multiplicity. We must make this known to our focal consciousness in a most simplistic way, because if we compare what's physically manifested to the ideal that's absolute, all that our intellect would reveal to us would be oxymoronical paradoxes. That's not to be taken negatively or in exhaustion, it's just the result of the infinite being explained by the finite. It cannot be fully explained without turning into empyreal, ethereal, and to the laymen, incomprehensible information. It's like having diplopia of the mind and one of the images is unrecognizable.

While I didn't plan on this work to be philosophical, there's always a need for logical rhetoric. I also wasn't planning on quoting everyone that's smarter than most, but again necessity dictates. The quote that I will now give to you has given me years of compelling thoughts that continue to fuel my journey. It is from the renown physicist Albert Einstein, and it reads, "Condemnation without investigation is the highest form of ignorance."

Our own cultures, rituals, regimens, habits, known and unknown, create prejudices and biases in us. They stagnate our growth and development towards Self so much till we are left weakened, vulnerable and susceptible to attack. Biases and prejudices are the creation of a condemnational mindset towards everything except what's thought to be yours or known to you by tradition. We hinder our own growth and development by not investigating. We get caught up in tradition so knowing Self isn't even possible and having true success in any area of life cannot be obtained. We fail Self, and therefore, we fail. We need to constantly prepare to be local, regional and global "Prometheans"; persistently ushering in great advancements for Self and life, and those who live it. That's what Einstein's quote would trigger in us if we actually applied it in a practical way.

Right now there's only tacticality being used by man. Have we really gone from being living spirits to artificial intelligence? Observing the world as a mechanical function doesn't speak the truth of a spirit being alive. It looks as if everything is waiting for something. Waiting to be activated, waiting to be re-validated, instead of living. We are supposed to be driven by life and the expression of living. That means to live in each moment, each right here, each right now. This immediate living is the highest form of the awareness of Self. It is not a new concept or a recent idea. This way of living is exactly how we were created to live; unless you are the result of a newborn infant who planned his Life Path. Life literally bubbles when we want to live, instead of waiting to live. We are refreshed perpetually when living. Joy becomes us, and that's not something even the greatest optimist really expects to see nowadays, and that's because Joy is Self, and the optimist just hasn't gotten that elevated yet.

Joy is not gladness, happiness or even glee. Joy is not based on riches or austerity. Joy is not practiced or exercised. Joy is that which manifests when an equal and balanced stillness is met or reached between the focal consciousness and Self. Joy is that which manifests when acceptance becomes a continuous state. Joy is the indifference obtained towards worldly objects. Joy dwells in the depth of nature that we wouldn't know of without Self. It is through a diversification in information, knowledge, overstanding and wisdom, that we call up Joy to dwell in our focal consciousness as Self.

What is it about the physical world that has us caught up in its rapture, other than its immediate results? Our bodies, being led by our egos, are ravenous for this form of attention. But it is fleeting, and comparable to an illusion or mirage of some type, because all things here must perish in their current state. When we begin to discover the longevity and recyclable nature of our material existence, the subatomic level of the universe, and learn of its essence, why would such a minuscule part of our existence be used to dictate the remains of infinity on us as good or painful? Unless, during that minuscule portion, the things done activate something that is extended beyond that time of temporality. There is something more being measured than just the physical aspect of ourselves.

How do you see the suggestions made in the preceding paragraph? Has it sunk in yet that there is more to us than what we normally think of or attribute to ourselves? We normally think of ourselves in a physical form in some type of relationship. We could be sons, fathers, brothers, daughters, mothers, sisters, friends, employees, etc. But if that is true, why then are temporary things capable of affecting us eternally? That wouldn't even be slightly fair. Thinking that we are physical manifestations only would certainly create confusion towards the one thing that most of the world believes exist, and that's an afterlife. Even if the atheist doesn't believe in God, the nothing he thinks is after this life has to become known to him as an afterlife in order for him to expect it. Which brings me right back to the question of… "how are the temporal things effective in infinity"?

The Self is that effective link of the temporal to the eternal, for it is the eternal self which does perceives temporal things, but is itself not perceivable by that which is temporal.

We're not totally against the physical world. The physical world is an intimate environment to be a part of, but knowing only it is stagnant to one's Heart of Mind. It becomes stale to only exist in the physical of life.

Since we have an eternal existence, whether it's in heaven, or hell, or nothing, it therefore speaks to our having eternal needs. Everyone and I do mean everyone, has those moments when we feel like there could be more to life, should be more to life, but we don't act on it. We return to the Rat Race and take up our regular, normal position. Even if we don't have lofty ambitions of the empyreal, it would be egregious to live a life that isn't full of living.

Even though we know about mind, thought, subjective, metaphysical, psychological, and idealistic attainments we are never given the full explanation of where these things exist, and what houses them. We have our imagination, but even that faculty becomes homeless when one attempts to describe its residence. In the society of the west, none of the common lifestyles even employ the concept of subconscious reality, mental activities of consciousness, and the physical abilities of mind. This can no longer be the case. The Self is where all of these intangible, but applicable, aptitudes reside, and also where they are fully functional. The Self is more psychological, more subjective, more idealistic, and more physical than any physical, manifested thing could ever reveal. It literally is the realm of cause to our physical effects. We wouldn't even be here if it wasn't for Self. For it was Self that called us into existence in the first place, and our reality is based on that initial beckoning.

What exactly is a beckoning, and what does it mean to us? A beckoning is a signaling, an invitation, a gesture, summons, or command. But what causes it is mystical. It seems to come from nowhere. It appears to be a part of the essence of our very Selves. It has been described as light that guides, a feeling that urges, or generally, intuition. But where our beckoning arises from is a place of Quietude; that Mystical Place of Peace. It's the one place where all things merge into a complete oneness, a still hum absent of any and all vibrations. What is known about quietude is that what is there is at the Alpha and Omega of all; of Stillness, of Oneness, of Unity, of Coalescing, of Singularity. This Quietude requires no injection of anything. Its achievement is the very opposite of injection. It's acquired not by injection but by removing from ourselves the mass and matter of this manifested world.

All over this earth we have a relativity towards all things. Depending on that relativity, at any time, we are beckoned into a thought triggered by that same object. Thoughts, identities, decisions, and circumstances are all products of that process. What we feel, relative to all other objects, dictates our perception of every aspect of ourselves, and of those objects once we are in that awareness.

So our relativity has to be changed to an equality of awareness. We must see all things from a balanced, unbiased, unprejudiced approach, so that a clearer perception and identity is made, creating proper knowledge, wisdom and awareness. This is all done in Quietude. Quietude happens when the focal consciousness is disconnected from stimuli, and not just from sights and sounds, but also from the way that we are affected by them. Once a moment of this magnitude of peace is attained, we are beckoned towards our duty. The call of Self naturally arises.

Our own internal experience is our Primary Reality. So that puts the Self up and out front. Meaning, if there is something to know about any individual it can be found in its cause here. But this realm requires a vision that's beyond the sight of our physical eyes, and beyond the hearing of our physical ears. That which we even think is known about seeing and hearing has to be re-thought and re-learned so that it is known of differently. The Self is in the category of being spiritual, ethereal, and even mystical, so it is not an intellectual process by any stretch of the imagination. It has all to do with our experiences, and we need to better take notice of this fact. Our own experience, and what we perceive from it, is the central issue.

Knowledge can only explain bits and parts, or fragments. Experience is what causes us to sense Self. Experience tunes us into the Self, and certain experiences are necessary in order for us to gain clarity and truth. We have to learn to see the true connections and relationships between things of all qualities and quantities, because everything is not as it appears to be.

Take for example an apple, is an apple the seed, the tree, or the fruit? We tack on adjectives and other nouns to apple in order to fully describe what we mean in any particular case, but again, what would we consider to be the ideal of an apply? So it is with man.

If we were to go back to any point in a search, wherever we may cease should still contain the origin of the initial reason for the search. We should not have strayed away from that which gave us our beckoning. But man has done this to man. Man has become amphoteric in these last days and times. With intoxicants and the fulfillment of fleshly desires, man seeks to experience the Euphoria of Self without the Attainment of Self. He wants the Eternalness of Self, but in the flesh. We cannot be amphoteric, partly one and partly another, in our lives. If that is attempted, then both shall stand in incompleteness, and man is complete. Most people think that their religion puts them in the arena of the eternal, but religion is particularly subdolous when addressing the eternal nowadays. The priest, ministers, preachers, imans, gurus and most leaders of a religious faction are mostly concerned with what's available and of concern right now, in the physical. Their rhetoric reflects that position, and therefore they teach an amphoteric way of belief and worship of the Celestial and Terrestrial. Man will not be partly in Heaven and partly on Earth. He will have to make the decision as to which God he serves. For it is either he discovers that which is eternal, and within, or not, and perish into oblivescence of that which is eternal.

Now let us talk about our observance of and unconfessing addiction to the advancement in technology, that is to us, most assuredly, a sybaritic disease that we fail to self-diagnose as a symptom of the illness of unrecognizing Self. There's a comfort, in the physical, in what we know of as advancement in technology. But knowing that any increase in physical comfort is a negation of spiritual development we are warned to wake up to this subdolous threat that heretofore was what gave us glee. Those who recognize Self don't practice physical austerities because they are depressed. The physical austerity that is seen of the higher developed beings here are just the tradeoff of the development of the Self, and what it really requires from this manifested world. What we think of as advancement in technology is no advancement at all. The things that are used for the advancement are fundamentals to life and have a primordial, primigenial positioning among the elements of creation, but we use them for the physical which negates any advancement.

We have become engulfed by the advancement in technology. To the point where it actually controls us. No one does anything without the assistance of or the association with some form of technology. Not even one of the most natural of our industries, agriculture, is without the services of technology. With this comes the terrible price of losing what it was that beckoned us to advance in technologies in the first place. The mind, intuition and creative imagination, withers under the weight of technological advancement, because technological advancements create a comfort that is cancerous to the struggle, trial, and tribulation of what we used to advance in technology. We need to feel the draw of necessity so that we move forward. But if there is a comfort that obstructs that path, we can never feel that draw of necessities.

Struggle is the ordained right of man and womanhood. There should never come a moment in time that either should feel as if they need not anything more of life. Life is to infinite to be regulated to any limit that creates sufficiency. We're not talking about infinite ecstasy in the technologies and sense pleasures, what's infinite in life, that should be sought, is the infinite overstanding of the Wisdom of Creation. Creation is Life, and in this we discover Self. Avoiding a hedonistic lifestyle can do nothing in the form of harm to us. We will never truly suffer from the vacancy of technology in our lives. In that deprivation, we gain a lucid view of the Self and all that is possible. Let no one and nothing become a killjoy to your discovery of, and intimacy with Self.

Do we suffer from a form of amnesia? A Spiritual amnesia of who we are, what we are, what are we doing here, and why are we even here in the first place? What could be the assignment, the obligation, of man that would sum up, and complete, all the who, what, and why's that define our existence in creations? What exactly was man commissioned to do while here on earth?

HOLY BIBLE REF. GENESIS 1-26 & PSALMS 8:6

Gen. 1:26

And God said, Let us make man in our image, after our likeness: and let them have dominion over the fish of the sea, and over the fowl of the air, and over the cattle, and over all the earth, and over every creeping thing that creepeth upon the earth.

Ps. 8:6

Thou madest him to have dominion over the works of thy hands; thou hast put all things under his feet.

HOLY QURAN REF. THE COW 2:30

The Cow 2:30

And when thy Lord said to the angels, I am going to place a ruler in the earth, they said: Wilt thou place in it such as make mischief in it and shed blood? And we celebrate Thy praise and extol Thy holiness. He said: Surely I know what you know not.

So many words describe our commission in existence. We know of a few general ones like love and create, but let us make an attempt at a fuller picture of purpose with the Latin Domin and Arabic Khalafa.

In order to have the sound ability and etiquette to carry out any of the definitions of the words used to describe our commission, one would have to possess a high distinguished form of rulership within himself. Not rulership over someone else, but rulership of Self and all of the attributes and characteristics of Self.

The Inner Self and how it expresses in the manifested world, according to the commission of Domin and Khalafa, has to be discovered, studied, and mastered. Mastery gives rulership. Rulership then must be transferred into our gift to life and its singularity. What we are doing when we reach the level of Domin and Khalafa is completing that final degree of divine assimilation of the image and likeness in being of God, and He being Serendipitous to us.

Master, owner, ruler, judge, and successor are all innate qualities that have to be realized by us in the capacity of Domin and Khalafa, and then brought up to an applicable level without the loss of Divine Purity. No causticity can be allowed to exist in the quality of Domin and Khalafa as we begin to accomplish them in ourselves. Self-Analyzation and Quality Analyzation will have to be constantly carried out so that the application of such abilities does what Divine Prominence has allocated them to be.

A master is a benefit to those under his hand by his mastery. An owner maintains and provides for that in which he owns. A ruler sets in place the limits of good or wicked behavior. A judge creates justice for him who has been dealt with unjustly. And a successor is one who takes from what he has been given and multiples that for an increase. These are only a few examples of the many characteristics of Domin and Khalafa that would be carried out, without limits, to fulfill the completeness necessary in our commission.

Since Divinity originates Domin and Khalafa, and Divine Purity has to be consistent in our applications, then essential knowledge must be the daily diet of the mind. Knowledge that penetrates the exterior of an object and drills deep within the subject is where the focus of our efforts must reside. No extent of an operation should be engineered without Divine Succor permeating it. No act or behavior can be performed in the absence of Divine Law, and no words or speech uttered without originating from Divine Sound. We need our "Vicissitude" to be activated so that we can journey back to our archetype of Divine Proficient Sapience, and not be to ourselves a Tyrannical Master.

There is a coadunational element within Domin and Khalafa that is apprehensible between all participants involved. The ones who know will work individually, but will feel a coalescing of purpose, and begin to satisfy that requirement of our commission. But every time either of these terms of rulership is mentioned, they are done so under the criteria that whoever it is, has already submitted to the Divine Authority that that rulership is given from. There is a subaudition received that allows for the Self to be aware of this command and the performance that it necessitates. This auspiciousness is well recognizable in our daily lives if we are unbound and unconfined to our manifested material world.

What Do You Know? Is It Real?

Addendum

Coalescing Knowledge

How, you may ask, is superior knowledge gained by those who realize that Life has a more Ultimate & Vast Meaning than We readily know? An accepting attitude is that first step in attempting to gain any knowledge, especially "Superior Wisdom". We will have to open Our Minds up to the unknown and different. We will have to venture into areas that may have produced phobias in Us. Fear is adverse to any form of elevation, enlightenment, or even balance. That is the concept that contributed to the Fall of Man, the degrading of cultures, and the Blind seeking of manifest desires. We need to empty what is full so that we can fill it with what is good. That's what We must do in order to make gains in "Superior Knowledge". Now We know, and so shall We do.

What will follow is a sample of how We look at subjects and words, that are being considered as increasers of knowledge and elevation and break into their constructions for an edifying effect.

The exegesis that We have given in "What Do You Know: Is It Real?" Comes from what we call "Coalescing Knowledge". It is overstanding gained by deciding on a subject, gathering all available information possible on that subject, no matter how exfoliated it is, or how distant it seems from the topic, defining as much and as many of the words, terms, and concepts that can be identified, and then creating a collage of coherence from that edification.

There are other systems that explain a process similar to this procedure. We coined Our particular one "Coalescing Knowledge", because, not only is the information brought together, but it is also nurtured so that a growing together can be achieved. We endeavor to make knowledge continue to be "Ever-Useful" throughout Our Journey in Life.

We will take a look at Worship, Prayer, Meditation, and Contemplation from the Coalescing Knowledge perspective using the Holy Bible, with the inclusion of Septuagint terms used by Greek Translators, and information otherwise known as possibly mystic.

No conclusion will be given in this sample for We leave all conclusions to the individual's experience and what may be viable to them. Our duty is to present the backdrop and all of its elaborations.

What a wonderful concept worship is. To exact one's Self onto an ideal and its attributes, feeling completely engulfed by its beauty and love, captures the "Purity of Belief". To worship brings the world to a standstill. A pause in this reality is created, so that a union can be made between the celestial and terrestrial. The higher and lower selves meet and resolve differences. The inner and external comes to a Oneness. The religious and spiritual finally agree.

Let's think about the "Purity of Belief" for a moment. How many have ever taken the opportunity to measure exactly what they believe in? In other words, who investigates and defines their object of worship, and its attributes, thoroughly? This would be a very critical area to dissect and analyze in one's life. It would possibly create a fear, paradox, or even doubt, concerning a strongly held position of belief. A whisper of uncertainty would reverberate capricious results. So on average, most do not have a "Purity of Belief" measured, only a feeble hope that they do.

It is taught that "what a person predominantly does is his worship". This is because worship causes all else to cease at its behest. A "Refulgent Thought" is manifested and the Life Continuum evaluates. Thought precedes action, so it is there that worship originates. No-thing can usurp its position of "Primus," and that is what makes it a "Worship" by practical definition. That Refulgent Thought is considered and contemplated until an inner dictate is issued. Committing the actions is then the ritual of worship, therefore rendering reality to that belief.

The union established between the celestial and terrestrial confirms "As above, so below." When the higher and lower selves meet, and resolve differences, a uniformity is created. Most worshipers do not know, nor realize, that there is a social order of rightness in the higher realms, that seeks its reflection in the lower realms. And because creation flows outwardly, the only way to see and know this is to look inwardly. Once an introspection is made, the inner and external will initiate coalescing; that will give True meaning and agreement between the religious and the spiritual.

Worship derives from the Saxon term "Worthship" and is used to indicate an attitude of homage. It is used in English to translate a Hebrew term in the O.T. that means "to bow or prostrate oneself," and a Greek term in the N.T. that means the same, but derives from a root meaning "to kiss".

325 A.D.
The Construction of an object of worship.

In the Nicene Creed, constructed at the Council of Nicaea, the counsel needed to affirm the essential unity of the Father and Son. The Council used a non-biblical term in that creed, for the first time. The compound word "Homousian", meaning in Greek, "of the same substance" equated the Son with the Father. This creed was held out to be a touchstone of orthodoxy, which it eventually became and continues to be to this day. It reads…

… "The only-begotten Son of God; Begotten of his Father before all worlds, God of God, Light of Light, Very God of Very God; Begotten, not made; Being of one substance (Homousian) with the Father; By whom all things were made"…

This continued the confirmation that whatever is worshiped is of the highest ideal, and guides and directs one in his entire life. In the case of the council of Nicaea, God manifested in the flesh of Him deserving worship, and so it had to be acknowledged and explained. In Our day and time, this fact still holds true concerning worship, but God, nor the Son, nor the manifestation of God is the subject or object. Idolatry, the works of the flesh, which leads to covetousness, is the usurper of this highest, life sustaining essence of deserving worship. This had to become known so that we realize why the world seems to be a worst place than it was a millennium ago.

Worship is an opportunity to express an internal process so that it may be witnessed. There is no worship without witness. The mental account and subjective reasonings that are had for an ideal cannot help but spill over from Our hearts, and minds, into Our bodies for expression. Man has always created or carried out the physical representation of his **noumena** in a ritual or regimen that describes or defines his endearment to that. The worship classification is made because of the total, overwhelming and consuming effect that are **noumenon** has on Us. It is, and is within, everything we consider and contemplate through thought, and so becomes the very essence, and way, of Our lives. So, what We do, pay attention to, practice, or commit application, is in fact, that which We worship. It begins in the mind, and it most certainly manifests in the physical world, for all to see. There is no worship without witness, therefore, whatever it is that is done or observed, in the majority, is worship or the object of it.

The intimacy that worship conjures up, in any practitioner, is more so than in any other aspect of their personal relationships, including erotic. There is no tighter bond, closer proximity, more concerning, willing to please, or deeper resentment against the enemies of that adored than in worship. Worship is the highest state of man. It is in worship that the decisions in one's life are ultimately and fundamentally made. Whatever it is that We worship, has its effect, has its influence in and over our lives. There is nothing done without the **Homogeneous** and essential nature of the object, or the **subjective noumena** of that which is worshiped, being in it as its main constituent of existence. You are what you desire, even if you haven't accomplished or acquired it.

One's success in the spirit has to dominate his desires. The **psychological hedonism** that this world possesses, is the poison for the destruction of the ideal of the True Self, the Spirit of Man. Having only a physical type of desire would make his worship null and void.

What is in Our life? What is it that We are carrying out as Our lives? If We analyze Our living in a true, keen and observant method, We will discover Our **Homoousion** or **Homoiousion,** that dictates Our thoughts and decisions in Our activities. This would explain Our Truth, and that would confirm Our Worship.

We know that to worship is to show a deep feeling of affection, an adoration. It helps one directs his focus and attention towards a single rightness. This single rightness is of the importance and dignity perceived in that which is worshiped. A worthiness is felt, and respect is given in mind, and in the body of the worshiper. Worship allows one to acknowledge an entity of standing or importance. Within worship is a form of religious practice, ritual, or regime with the possibility of creed or song.

Worship also speaks to the reverence paid to a divine being. This reverence is a feeling of profound awe and love that is unparalleled towards anything else known to the worshiper. Bowing and prostration are the physical actions that come from this aspect of worship. The revering nature that worship creates promotes the veneration of that entity. Here is where We will begin an investigation into the areas that promote reverence up to a physical action. These actions are known to us under the description of prayer.

It is known to Us, without a doubt, that "half the story has never been told," and when We say this we mean it literally, not figuratively! We've been continuously given a very broad view of God, religion, spirituality, mysticism, esoterica, exoteria, physics, science, and life in general. We are not taught complete and thorough, comprehensive and overstood, systemic and organized ways of anything in these days and time. The considerations due towards education and intelligence have been usurped by pleasure seeking. The teachers have gone away from the knowledge and wisdom of the components and elements that would give Us a fullness of Way. The details are what eludes Us all.

That brings Us to the topic of this writing, "What is Prayer"? By today's standard, the ancients wouldn't even consider what We do as prayer, prayer. What was once a remarkable elaborate, intimate, fully stimulating, spiritual and mystical act, and experience, has now become some exorbitant exfoliation of the only true glorious act that man can perform. No other duty can rank higher to man than true prayer.

But if We want to truly know prayer, We have to go back to where prayer originated from. That would take Us to contemplation, and that would bring Us to meditation. Meditation is the origin of prayer. It is the Father of it, and that in which prayer is begotten from. So We must first know meditation, or rather its root, meditate.

<u>MEDITATION</u>

To Meditate means to ponder or reflect on; to consider; to plan or project in the mind; design in thought; or engage in studious reflection. In doing so, meditation then allows Us to devote, in private, or as a spiritual exercise, Our cognitive abilities to subjective concepts. A steady and close consecutive reflection and continued application of the mind then keeps Us on a course of replenishment for Our overall health.

The methodical reflection, deep thought on eternal truth, which becomes a religious exercise, because of its spiritual goals and reverent approach, causes meditation to play a role in all religions, ancient and modern, major and minor; from the farthest places East to the nearest locations West, and in all denominations.

Meditation is called discursive prayer or mental prayer. In the Eastern Orthodox Ideal meditation is engaged in for seeking deeper insight into the Will of God. Meditation, by whomever practiced, is an attempt to still the ordinary thoughts of the human mind, to explore the depth, and if possible, to break through the bondage of the finite into the infinite.

When the scriptures were translated into the Greek, there wasn't an equivalent conceptual word for the ancient idea of meditation. But since, in the ancient sense, meditation was supposed to engulf one's life as the practice of it increased, the Greek word that would best define this practice was the one that means "to watch over, protect," this word is ter'eo. It is where We must identify how this concept was shifted into a transition down to Our modern overstanding, here are the declensions: **Teresis** [to watch over, protect], **teresis** [watch, custody], **paretereo** [to watch closely, guard], **parateresis** [watching, observance], **diatereo** [to keep, store up], **Syntereo** [to keep in mind, protect].

The basic meaning of this word is to keep in view, to note, to watch over; it takes on such nuonces as to rule, to observe, to ward off, to guard, to keep, and in a transferred sense, to see to, to apply oneself to, to defend oneself. The word occurs 39 times in the Septuagint; in such senses as to aim at, to keep watch, to pay attention, to watch over or for, to keep, to observe. In the NT, the literal meaning is used 60 times. Tereo may have here such literal senses as to guard (Acts 12:6; Mt. 27:36), to keep (Jn. 2:10; 1 Pet. 1:4), to retain (negatively in Jude 6), and to protect (1 Cor. 7:37).

The sense is to protect or to preserve in Jn. 17: 11-12. So too, Christ protects his church against temptation in Rev. 3:10. Paul's desire is that the spirits, souls, and bodies of believers may be kept (with an eschatological reference) in 1 Th. 5:23. The called will be kept for the reign of Christ in Jude. Christ grants protection against the devil and sin in 1 Jn. 5:18. Keeping aloof from the world is the point in 1 Tim. 5:22 and Jms. 1:27. In Jude 21 the genitive ("of God") expresses God's initiative, the verb Our response.

With an impersonal object, the idea is that of maintaining the essential Christian realities, e.g., faith in 2 Tim. 4:7, the unity of the Spirit in Eph. 4:3, and one's garments (e.g., salvation) in Rev. 16:15. A common thought is that of observing or keeping commandments Mt. 19:17; Acts 15:5; Jn. 9:16 (the Sabbath); Mt. 23.3 (scribal teachings); Jms. 2:10 (the royal law); Mt. 28:20 (Yeshua's teachings); Jn. 14:15 (Yeshua's commandments). The expressions used relative to Christians suggest the existence of a catechetical tradition. This goes back to the teaching of Yeshua himself so that keeping his commands is the same as keeping his word (Jn. 14:23-24). The disciples pass on this word of revelation with a summons of faith and obedience (Jn. 15:20), and keeping it means eternal life (Jn. 8: 51-52). Similar thoughts occur in 1 Jn. 2:3-4; Rev. 12:17. The Christian life, as a fulfilling of God's Will, is both a prerequisite of answers to prayers and a result of the Spirit's working (1 Jn. 3:22,24). Love for God finds expression in the love for others, and in keeping the commandments (Jn.5:2-3).

Tereis. In Greek, this word means attention, vigilance, watch, observation, preservation, care, and custody. In the Septuagint it occurs only in the Apocrypha for keeping or guarding. In the NT, the words mean custody (or prison) in Acts 4:3; 5:18, and keeping or fulfilling God's commandments in 1 Cor. 7:19, Gal. 5:6; Rom. 14:17.

Paratereo. In Greek, this word has such senses as to observe, to keep under observation, to lurk, to lie in wait, to pay heed, to note, to be on the lookout, to preserve, to watch over and keep. In the Septuagint, the verb means to lurk, in Ps. 37:12, of and to keep in mind, in Ps. 130:3. In other Jewish Greek works one finds the sense to find by observation, to wait for observantly, and to observe (cultic regulations). In the NT, paratereo means to watch in Mk. 3:2, and to guard (the gates) in Acts 9:24. Cultic observance is the point in Gal. 4:10. A relapse into the observance of days entails a loss of freedom. Paul may be arguing here against compulsory keeping of the Sabbath and OT feasts, but he may also be rejecting the idea of lucky or unlucky days and seasons, for the compound (in the middle) suggest anxious observance in one's own interest.

Parateresis. In Greek this means watching, lying in wait, spying, attention, scrutiny, scientific observation, self-scrutiny, self-discipline, watching over, keeping (law etc.), observing (usage), and maintaining (obedience). In the NT, it occurs only in Lk. 17:20, where it might have either a temporal or a local reference (observing times or places). These are linked in apocalyptic writings. The statement that the kingdom is among you or in your midst suggests, not that the calculation of signs in contrasted with some future incursion of the kingdom, but that the kingdom has already come in Yeshua. Some people, however, do not perceive it. Observation of signs cannot show whether the kingdom has come, as it is now at work, for God's rule can be grasped only by faith. The messianic expectations of the opponents of Yeshua, who are demanding signs, are wholly inadequate in the face of what Yeshua effects with his coming among the people.

Diatereo. In the NT, this word occurs in Lk. 2:51 for keeping or storing up in the memory. The sense in Acts 15:29 is to keep oneself, to abstain.

Syntereo. This word means to keep in the memory in Lk. 2:19, to protect in Mk. 6:20, to be preserved in Mt. 9:17.

On the highest levels and degrees, of All Belief Systems, meditation is urged and seen as necessary for the development of faith, and a deep comprehension of life, and its needs. Meditation is a steadying and continuing exercise, and it is because of this nature that most of the populace find it difficult to perform. The powers that be, intentionally or not, maliciously or not, saw this as an optionary right for the congregation or the uninitiated; so the populace was given a compromise of lesser obligation (i.e. prayer). The non-requiredness for the congregation, or the uninitiated, was due to the length of time that meditation used in its operation. Anywhere from a few hours to days or weeks is the normal range for the time one may need to meditate. To gain entry into the state of stillness, that is the objective of meditation, may have several layers of processing necessitated upon it. To remove the attentiveness that We have for sense stimuli is of the first order. Next, would be the silencing of Our own internal dialogue. Then, as We begin to focus more intently, We still have to smooth out the kaleidoscope of information, sights, sounds and feelings that are characteristics of meditation, but not fully comprehensible. All of this has no relativity to time. In the ascension into meditation, time begins to lose its nature with the meditator. It is no longer the numerable aspect of motion, or the reality that is an absolute flowing apart from the events filling it, but becomes a priori form of inner sensible intuitions that have no existence independently of the mind, and are a subjective mode in which phenomena appears. This is the reason why distance seems to disappear during meditation. We go from one place to another, which aren't normally near one another, in immediacy, taking no time in covering vastness. It is also why We can be in any part of Our lives, past, present, or future. Nothing about time limits the true meditator. Once one reaches this state, needs and necessities, wants and desires, all become obtainable. It is why the Ancients were always able to fulfill any duty that presented itself to them. Every obligation was met through the practice and exercise of meditation. But, as populations grew, so did incorrect behavior and deviation from the True Way. "Pleasure Principles" became the gods of the people, and the Living God was abandoned by the masses. So, in an effort to begin the process of turning the masses back to the living God, before judgment ensued, a lesser regimen of spiritual behavior was implemented, as an initial step, into the full recovery of lost souls in this physical world.

Having full recovery of Our souls is identifying with what is deemed purposeful in life eternal. What We know of, as the purpose of meditation is the "Mete". To Mete is to find the value, measure, or worth in a thing. It is also to find the quantity, dimension, or capacity of by any rule or standard; to determine the value of or appraise. So We find a science within meditation that contributes to the art and tactical application of it towards, and gives one, prominence.

Meditation is what prayer ultimately is! We just haven't been taught this in a very long time. The thing is, though, We didn't go from meditation straight to prayer. We made a stop in what we call contemplation, so let's see what the qualities of it is.

Contemplation, which resembles meditation, is a variant in that it seeks a mystical experience, rather than the relaxation in the spiritual, or the awareness of the spiritual, by concentrating only on a particular object of worship; be it a script, image, symbol, or sound. Based on the etymon of the linguistic construction of contemplation, it is correct to say that contemplation is a joining in space and time, with an object of the physical world, in Our mental capacity. In other words, it is a severe and astonishing mental projection into the essential nature of, and soon thereafter, the meaning of an object of symbolic, linguistic form, or idealistic presence, in one's life.

Contemplation is a devotional exercise that captures wavering thoughts and removes their hindrances so that a focal consciousness can be obtained towards Our private, individual, spiritual affairs. It creates for Us a state in tuned with the mystic awareness of God's being. It is Our ethereal bridge.

In ancient times, contemplation was the skill used to foretell the immediate future. When We read of those performing magical prowess, in the folklores and myths, it was through contemplation that they gained the insight, knowledge, and even abilities that they became renowned for.

Today, because Our way of life is not in line with the spiritual, We have to become attuned to Our higher frequency. Contemplation deepens this tuning and aligns this channeling clearer than the prayer perspective. Once the channel is certainly opened, and a height is reached, with a purpose caused, and distinguished from the rest of the world, Our merits begin the unlocking of the gates that they have the keys to. Each gate allows for the elevation that gives us the deeper experience produced therein. That makes each gate tremendously valuable in what is necessary for spiritual development.

In the midst of contemplation is a transition from sensory to intellectual, to spiritual perception. A distinction is sometimes made between acquired, active, and ordinary contemplation and that which is infused, passive and extraordinary.

Infused, passive and extraordinary contemplation refers to the higher states of the mystical life. It is the union that is spoken of, and sought after, by the most faithful. The distinction between this and the prayer of loving attention is a special gift and vocation. This extraordinary contemplation was well on its way to prominence with a second wave of distinction up until the 14th century. There in the mid-1300's a stifling blow was made to contemplation in the Hesychasm controversy.

HESYCHASM, a form of MYSTICISM prevalent on Mount Athos in the fourteenth century. The term "hesychasm" is derived from the Greek word for "silence" since the hesychasts practiced sitting in silence for long periods. One of the earlier hesychasts, Gregory of Sinai, recommended sitting with the chin resting on the chest, looking at one's navel, and holding one's breath as long as possible while repeating "Lord Yeshua Christ, have mercy on me." This drew the ridicule of some, who also supported closer ties with the Western church, and therefore the controversy over hesychasm soon became also a controversy over relations with the West. Gregory Palamas, one of the foremost Byzantine theologians of the time, came to the support of Hesychasm, although not of its more extreme practices, and in 1351 a council declared itself in favor of Hesychasm as an approved method of contemplation and condemned those who had ridiculed it.

Under church tradition, the practice of Hesychasm has its beginnings in the bible, Matthew 6:6 and in the

Philokalia. The tradition of contemplation, with inner silence or tranquility, is shared by all Eastern ascenticism having its roots in the Egyptian traditions of monasticism exemplified by such Orthodox monastics as St. Anthony of Egypt. About the year 1337, Hesychasm attracted the attention of a learned member of the Orthodox Church, Barlaam, a Calabrain monk who at the time held the office of Abbot in the monastery of St. Saviors' in Constantinople, and who visited Mount Athos. There, Barlaam encountered Hesychasts and heard descriptions of their practices, and also read the writings of the teacher in Hesychasm, St. Gregory Palamas, himself a monk. Hesychasm, according to St. Gregory Palamas, is a form of constant purposeful prayer or experiential prayer, explicitly referred to as "Contemplation". It is to focus one's mind on God and pray to God unceasingly. The Hesychasts stated that at higher stages of their prayer practice they reached the actual contemplation-union with the Tabor Light, i.e. Uncreated Divine Light, or Photomos; seen by the Apostles in the event of the Transfiguration of Christ, and Saint Paul while on the road to Damascus. It is depicted in icons and theological discourse also as tongues of fire.

    Trained in Scholastic theology, Barlaam was scandalized by Hesychasm and began to campaign against it. As a teacher of theology, in the Scholastic mode, Barlaam propounded a more intellectual and propositional approach to the knowledge of God than the Hesychasts taught. In particular, Barlaam took exception to, as heretical and blasphemous, the doctrine entertained by the

Hesychasts as to the nature of the uncreated light, the experience of which was said to be the goal of Hesychast practice. It was maintained by the Hesychasts to be of divine origin and to be identical to that light which had been manifested to the disciples on Mount Tabor at the Transfiguration. Barlaam held this concept to be polytheistic, inasmuch as it postulated two eternal substances, a visible immanent and an invisible God transcendent.

On the Hesychast side, the controversy was taken up by St. Gregory Palamas, afterwards Archbishop of Thessalonica, who was asked by his fellow monks on Mt. Athos to defend Hesychasm from Barlaam's attack. St. Gregory was well-educated in Greek Philosophy, dialectical method, and thus able to defend Hesychasm. In the 1340's he defended Hesychasm at three different synods in Constantinople and also wrote a number of works in its defense.

In 1341 the dispute came before a synod held at Constantinople and was presided over by the Emperor Andronicus. The synod, taking into account the regard in which the writings of Pseudo-Dionysius were held, condemned Barlaam, who recanted and returned to Calabria, afterward becoming a bishop in the Roman Catholic Church. Three other synods on the subject were held, at the second of which the followers of Barlaam gained a brief victory, but in 1351 at the synod under the presidency of the Emperor John VI Cantacuzenus, Hesychast doctrine, and Palamas' Essence-Energies distinction, was established as the doctrine of the Orthodox Church.

One of Barlaam's friends, Gregory Akindynos, who originally was also a friend of Gregory's, later works took up the controversy. Another opponent of Palamism was Manuel Kalekas who sought to reconcile the Eastern and Western Churches. Following the decision of 1351, there was strong repression against anti-Palamist thinkers. Kalekas reports on this repression as late as 1397, and for theologians in disagreement with Palamas, there was ultimately no choice but to emigrate and convert to Catholicism, a path taken by Kalekas as well as Demetrios Kydones, and Ioannes Kypariossiotes. This exodus of highly educated Greek scholars, later reinforced by refugees following the Fall of Constantinople in 1453, had a significant influence on the first generation, that of Petrarca and Boccaccio, of the incipient Italian Renaissance.

Contemplation = com, col, con, or cor L, = with, together: jointly + template fr. Templum = space for observation. This word came down to us from a group of Greek terms including; **horao** [to see, perceive], **eidon** [to see, perceive, visit], **bleop** [to see, watch], **optanomia** [to appear], **theamonia** [to behold], **theoreo** [to view, contemplate], **aoratos** [invisible], **haratos** [visible], **horasis** [sight, vision], **hormana** [vision], **optasia** [appearing], **autoptes** [eyewitness], **epoptes** [spectator, overseer], **epopteus** [to view, inspect], **ophthalmos** [eye, apple of the eye], **kathorao** [to see, perceive], **proorao** [to foresee], **proeidon** [to foresee].

While akauo is virtually the only Greek word for hearing, there are various words for seeing. The first of these is horao, which means to look, to see, to experience, to perceive, to take note, to see to, to take care. The range of "eidon" is much the same.

Blepo also means to see with a stronger emphasis on the function of the eye, so that it serves as the opposite of to be blind. It can also be used for intellectual or spiritual perception, and in the absolute for insight.

Optanomai is rare and late and has the sense to be visible, to appear.

Theaomai suggests spectators and denotes attentive seeing, i.e., to behold. Having a certain solemnity, it is used for visionary seeing and apprehension of higher realities.

Theoreo has primary reference to spectators at a religious festival, and thus means to look at, to view, with such additional senses as to review troops, to discover, to recognize, and figuratively to consider, to contemplate, to investigate.

The Greeks are a people of the eye and seeing is important to them. It has a strong significance in their religion, which is a religion of vision. If theoreo is derived from theos, and first means watching over the god, this is even more true, but that derivation is unlikely. Quite early there is a transition from sensory to intellectual and spiritual perception. The two are seen to be linked, but there is also a sense of the limits of sensory seeing.

Mythology allows that the gods can be seen, but only in a visionary manner to a few, and then in a frightening way. Philosophy stresses the invisibility of the gods, and Plato with his world of ideas finds an antithesis between horan and neoin. True reality is accessible only to the nous; this alone can comprehend God. Yet this comprehension is still viewed as a kind of seeing, especially in the form of theorin.

For Aristotle seeing is the most spiritual sense, since it gives access to light. As Plato thinks that we contemplate God with the eye of the soul, so for Aristotle the true goal of life is contemplative Self-Giving to God, for God's own mode of being and working consists of pure theoria. The divine is something to be contemplated, not heard and believed. Thus, philosophy transposes into an intellectual key something that is a historical reality in Greek religion. The visual is important in the mysteries as well. True bliss is to see the rites and enjoy visionary experiences.

Gnosticism accepts the invisibility of God but believes that deification by gnosis brings the vision of God. In the Hermetic writings, this comes only with death, although it may be possible in this life for a few Gnostics. Hearing the teacher is merely a preparation for ecstatic vision. In magical papyri formulas, actions are offered for forcing gods and demons to manifest themselves, and thus come under control.

With eidon (930 times), horao (520 times) covers most of the references to seeing. The future opsomia is common (178 times), while present (110) and perfect (97) are balanced. The main Hebrew original for both verbs is ra'ah (over 400 times for horao, and 670 times for eidon).

Figuratively, water, the sea, and the earth, may be to

see, Ps. 77:16; 114:3; 97:4. The dead will never again see the light, Ps. 49:19. When seeing and hearing occur together, the reference is usually to recognition or understanding, Job 13:1. Either may come first, for God has created both, Prov. 20:12. Yet seeing may be contrasted with mere hearsay, Ps. 48:8. In the intransitive passive sense (to show oneself, to appear), the meaning is usually to be present (the fixed expression to appear before God). The thought of seeing God's face is rare, Ex. 33:30, and LXX normally has in view a spiritual encounter, Ps. 17:15.

In ordinary use seeing the face usually means to visit, to meet, or at court, to be granted an audience. Horao and eidon often denote spiritual perception in such sense as to observe, Gen. 16: 4-5, to perceive, 26:28, to experience, Jer. 5:12, and to encounter (God's works in history), Ex. 34:10. Thus seeing God's Glory means receiving the revelation of God in his Glory, Ps. 97:6; Is. 26:10. The more concrete ophthenoa is used in Ex. 16:10 because the glory appears in a cloud, but the cloud is only a veil so that the verb denotes the presence itself, not the manner of the presence. The parallelism of Ex. 16:6 and 16:7 (to know and to see the glory) shows that sensory perception of the glory is not the issue, Is. 40:5.

Blepo occurs over 130 times, 38 in Ezekiel (35 of those for the geographical and architectural directions; Num. 21:20; Josh. 18:14). In the main, the Hebrew original is the same as for horao. Ability to see is mostly in view, including the ability to perceive. God is the subject in Ps. 10:11. Prophetic vision is an issue in Am. 8:2; Zach. 4:2; 5:2.

Optanomai is rare. It occurs in 1 Kgs. 8:8 (the poles could not be seen from outside). We also find the intransitive passive in Num. 14:14 (God is seen).

Theaomai occurs eight times (with a Hebrew original only in 2 Chr. 22:6; to visit). The sense is that of seeing with astonishment, of contemplating God's acts, and of seeing Jerusalem's future glory.

Theoreo occurs some 56 times, often with other verbs of seeing as alternative readings. In Daniel (13 times) the reference is usually to visionary seeing, but sense perception is the point in Josh. 8:20; Judg. 13: 9-10, and to live is what is meant in Eccl. 7:11. Watching as a spectator is the meaning in Judge. 16:27 and Ps. 68:24. Actual seeing is less prominent in Ps. 73:3, but only in Wis. 6:12; 13:5 does the term mean to perceive.

The Significance of Seeing in OT Proclamation: As regards the distinction between sensory and spiritual seeing, the compass of verbs of seeing is much the same in Greek and Hebrew. When God is said to see, sensory perception is not in view; there are few anthropomorphisms in the narrower sense, Gen. 6:12; Ex. 12:13, for it is only poetically that the Psalms and prophets refer to God's seeing. The verbs of seeing, like those of hearing, embrace many meanings that have little to do with actual seeing, although in the main it seems that, in the relationship with God and his revelation, hearing is regarded as more important than seeing. The main uses are as follows…

Visionary Prophetic Seeing. Horao and eidon are the words of prophetic visions. Prophets are called seers, and for this term horasis or hormana is used in 2 Sam. 24:11; 2 Kgs. 17:3, etc. The OT, however, does not record visions in the case of the seers; their revelations are by word, 2 Sam. 24:11. The dreams in Gen. 37:9, are purely visual and need interpretation. If they are accepted as impartations of the divine will, they are not manifestations of God. The visions of Zechariah are inner perceptions. The mark of authentic visions is that in them the prophets are recipients, not authors; they cannot induce them by prayer, sacrifice, etc. There is no specific term for audition, and horasis may apply to more than visual elements, possibly because seeing is more important at first, then yields to hearing as the great prophets hear God's own word but never see God Himself in their visions, only creatures or creaturely processes. Ezekiel sees the glory of God but does not describe it. Dan. 7:8 mentions the Ancient of Days but again without description; for the fate of the empires is the real point of the vision. Am. 9:1 is purely introductory. If Is. 6:1 is unique, here again, there is no description, and in 1 Kgs. 22:19 the real reference is to the True Word of God that Micaiah is to deliver to Ahab.

Theophanies. Num. 12:6-8 makes it plain that there is a difference between prophetic vision and the most direct theophany in Moses' case. Yet even Moses does not see God directly, Ex. 33:1. In Ex. 3:2 the angel (or God himself) appears to Moses in the bush, but Moses veils his face, and if 3:16 says that God has appeared to him, this simply means that he has manifested himself as present, as also to Abraham. In Ex. 24:10 a select group ascends the mountain and sees God, but the LXX softens the realism. In Ex. 33:18 the basic principle is that to see God directly is to die because of the divine holiness; hence Moses is permitted only an indirect vision. The same principle appears in Ex. 19:21, and Gen. 32:30; Judg. 6:22, where it is only by God's special grace that the rule does not apply. In instances like Gen. 12:7; 17:1, God is simply heard, and the introductory ophthenai indicates the presence of the God who reveals Himself in His Word. These are not, then, attenuated theophanies.

Sense. Often seeing God is in a transferred sense. Thus Ps. 17:15 refers to the certainty of God's proximity, while in Sir. 15:7 the meaning is perception. In Job 23:9 Job sees no sign that God is taking note of him, in 34:29 seeing God means certainty of His grace, and in 42:5 the reference is to spiritual understanding. Job 19:26-27 raises the question of seeing God after death. Job 23:9 and 35:14 suggest that the point might be seeing God's grace again in this life, but even if the reference is to the future the idea is probably that God's grace still sustains Job after death. In Is. 60:2 there will be a future vision of the divine glory, but again with reference more to God's revealing presence than to the eschatological vision.

Horao (with eidon) is for Philo the most important verb of seeing. The future and the passive are rare, and there is ophthenai of God only in OT quotations. Horao may denote sensory seeing (except in the case of God), but its main use is for spiritual perception. The words and voice of God are visible in this sense, and horao (with theoreo) may thus be used for "seeing" God. Blepo has primary reference to sense perception and is seldom used of God. Theaomai is used for intensive looking and occurs in relation to visions and seeing God. Theoreo mostly means to consider, to perceive, and passively to show. Theoria is common for perception and also as the opposite of praxia while theorem (almost always plural) had the meaning view or doctrine.

The Significance of Seeing. Adopting Plato's dualism, Philo has a poor view of the senses. The chief of these is seeing and hearing. Seeing as perception of the noetic world is superior to hearing, but as an agent in human development, not as a response to revelation. Does this mean that Philo has in view a vision of God? His exposition of the OT passages is inconclusive, and his references to deification and vision are counterbalanced by references to the divine invisibility and unknowability. Since the latter references are more common, and Philo says that we see only the fact and not the nature of God's existence, he seems to speak of the vision of God only with qualifications.

In Josephus, the primary emphasis is on sensory seeing and the related mental perceptions. Blepo and theoreo are less common; the former is often used figuratively for to note, to observe, while the latter signifies to view (as a witness), to be present (as a spectator). When directions are received in dreams, this is not seeing God, for God is intrinsically invisible for Josephus.

The Pseudepigrapha. In apocalyptic writing seeing is important, but angels explain the visions so that hearing is the climax. Even when God is seen, as in Eth. En. 14:15, this leads up to God's word. The vision of God is not an end in itself. God's glory is seen in heavenly wonders. The eschatological vision hinted at in places is visions of God's glory, or face, or salvation. In Jub. 1:28 God will appear to all eyes in the last time.

The rabbis lay the stress on hearing, as the OT does. They are thus opposed to the idea of ecstatic vision. At most they speak of seeing the face of Shekinah. This is an eschatological vision, but it may come in the days of the Messiah. God himself is invisible so that even angels cannot see Him. Reading the face of the Shekinah may take place in this life through attending the temple or synagogue, studying the law, or giving alms.

In the NT harao and eidon are the most common verbs of seeing. The former occurs some 113 times, the latter some 350 times in the Gospels, Acts, and Revelation. Eidon is less common in John, mainly because the perfect heoraka is preferred. John uses theoreo instead of the present harao, which is generally uncommon, being replaced elsewhere by blepo. The two verbs horao and eidon have a broad range of meaning. God is said to "see" in Acts 7:34. Harao is used for seeing Christ in Jn 3:11; 6:46; 8:38. To see means to speak to in Jn. 12:21. The distinction in Phil. 1:27, 30 does not imply any antithesis between seeing and hearing, and if seeing is more highly estimated in Jn. 8:38, seeing and hearing constitute the totality of perception in Mk. 4:12; Mt. 13:14-15; Acts 28:26-27; and Rom. 11:8. For the most part, seeing comes first in such cases, but hearing is first in Lk. 2:20; and Jn.

5:37. Seeing alone is mentioned in Jn. 12:40 and Rom. 11:10. Seeing signs is equivalent to hearing the message in Acts 8:6 and Jn. 11:45 but the desire to see signs may also denote resistance to the message, Mt. 12: 38; Lk. 23: 8. Often the verbs mean to perceive in such senses as to experience, to note, to establish, to realize, to know, to judge, to mark, to heed.

Blepo occurs some 137 times, mostly in the present. It first denotes the ability to see as distinct from blindness, Mt. 12:22; 15:31; Mk. 8: 23-24; Lk. 7:21; Jn. 9. Seeing the book in Revelations 5:3-4 includes reading. Scrutiny is implied in Mt. 22:16. God's seeing in Mt. 6:4 is a secret one. Eusus sees the Father's works in Jn. 5:19, 8:38. Angels see the face of God in Mt. 18:10. Empirical seeing is the point in Rom. 8:24-25; 2 Cor. 4:18; Heb. 11: 1. Figuratively blepo can mean to note, to perceive, Rom. 7:23; Col. 2:5. It is rare for the visionary seeing, Acts 12:9; Rev. 1:11-12. It is not used for appearance of the risen Lord or for eschatological vision. In Acts 1:9, 11 it denotes full participation rather than mere sensory perception. In 1 Cor. 13:12 the image of the mirror shows that the use is metaphorical, even in the second half of the statement, which also does not mention God as the object. Only in Mt. 18:10 and Jn. 5: 19 is blepein used for seeing God.

Optanomai, this word occurs only in Acts 1:3 with reference to the resurrection appearances. It is used because an appearing comprising many proofs demands a present participle.

Theaomai occurs 22 times. It suggests a more intimate visit in Rom. 15:24 (compared to idein in 1:11). It means "to look over" in Mt. 22:11, is more graphic than idein in 11: 7-8, stresses the element of loving regard in 28:1, and brings out the importance of the meeting in Lk. 5:27. Attentive regard is implied in acts 21:27. The use in John has a certain solemnity in 6:5, and the same applies in 1:14, where it denotes not just the seeing of witness but the seeing of faith. Theaomai is never used in the NT for seeing God.

Theoreo occurs 58 times (24 in John and 14 in Acts). In John, the present theoreo seems to be used instead of horao. It has the original sense to watch in Mt. 27:55. The chief sense in Acts is to perceive, 4:13, 17:16; In Jn. 6:19, 20:6, 12, 14. Sense perception is at issue, but to perceive or recognize is the point in 4:19, 12:9, and to know or experience in 8:51, and possible in 17:24 in an eschatological sense.

Generally, as in the Septuagint, there are in the NT more instances of verbs of seeing (680) than of hearing (425), yet hearing is more important. The NT has little interest in the physiology or psychology of seeing, and since it makes no distinction between the sensory and the spiritual, it readily accepts seeing as a function in revelation. If more blind people than deaf people are healed in the Gospels (Mt. 9:27; Mk. 8:22-23, etc.), this is most likely because eye afflictions are more common, not because sight is more important or Yeshua wants eyewitnesses.

Eyewitness: Faith and Sight. Mt. 13:16 seems to command eyewitness, but the reference to eyes and ears, Lk. 11:27 does not necessarily stress sense perception. The point is rather that those who have the privilege of seeing and hearing should not fail to attain to True seeing and hearing, Mt. 13:14-15. Underlying the saying is the conviction that the age of salvation has come with Yeshua, and that a right decision must be made in light of it. Lk. 1:2 basis the truth of the gospel on a tradition that goes back to eyewitnesses. Eyewitness here includes ministry of the word and thus comprises both seeing what took place and understanding its significance as revelation, Jn. 20:31. It is authentic then, only when the imperative of faith is present as well as the privilege of sight. The stress on eyewitness in 2 Pet. 1:18 is unusual, and the statements in Jn. 1:14 and 1 Jn. 1:1 includes more than eyewitness, for what follows is no mere report but proclamation. The Gospels omit many details (the appearance of Yeshua, scenery, etc.), for their focus, is on the words (hearing) and acts (seeing) of Yeshua. Word and work (hearing and seeing) constitute the full historicity and totality of the event of revelation. Hearing is primary, but seeing is a kind of hearing, for if dependence on a certain kind of seeing is unbelief, Mk. 15:32, then seeing too can and should lead to faith, Jn. 11:40. In Jn. 20:24, while the reference is to seeing the risen Lord, the statement in v. 29 has more general validity. As the first eyewitness is oriented to proclamation, so proclamation rest on the first eyewitness as a safeguard of historicity. Thus, the seeing of the disciples becomes the hearing of later believers, 1 Cor. 15: 3; Rom. 10: 16. It is no longer essential that those who preach the gospel should be themselves, witnesses. A contrast arises between what is seen and what is not seen 2

Cor. 4:18. What is seen is perishing, but what is not seen- and this includes not merely what is yet to come but inner renewal by the operation of the Spirit and the powers of the coming age is eternal. Similarly, the object of faith and hope in Rom. 8: 24-25 is not yet seen, for otherwise faith and hope would be unnecessary. Believers have a present sonship in faith, but they are still hoping for eschatological sonship as a visible entity. In Heb. 11:1 the things not seen, qualifying the things hoped for, are future things. Incidental contrast is the visible world of v. 3, which is created, as faith perceives, by the nonvisible word of God.

Visionary Prophetic Seeing or Dream-revelations are rare in the NT. In Mt. 1: 20, Joseph is given verbal directions by the angel so that these are not true visions. The same applies in Lk. 1:11; Acts 7: 2-3; 9:10; 18: 9; 23: 11. God does not speak directly here, as in OT parallels, but either an angel or the Lord, Acts 9:10. There is no ecstatic element, nor are there any theophanies except in the quotation in Acts 7: 2. A voice speaks in Mt. 3: 17 and parallels, but only in Acts 7: 31 do we have direct mention of the voice of God. Angels appear in the infancy stories (Lk. 1: 11-12), but only as heralds of the divine action. In Lk. 22: 43-44 the appearing of the angel simply implies that an angel comes in to help Yeshua, not that he has a vision of an angel.

In the resurrection stories, angels are seen again, this time as agents of proclamation. Jn. 20:12 is the only angelophony in John (unless we include the thunder of 12: 29). Acts 1: 10 belongs to the resurrection group. The angel that comes to Cornelius in 10:3 bears a message. In

5: 19-20; 12:7 angels bring release from prison and explanatory messages. 12:9 shows that what takes place is real even though it belongs to the suprasensory realm. In Acts 10:10 we are specifically told that Peter is in a trance so that we have a parallel to the prophetic visions of the OT.

Visions of future events occur in Revelation, but we learn from Rev. 1:3; 22:7, that what is intended is prophecy rather than apocalyptic, and in the last analysis the word predominates, 22: 6, 8. Paul has ecstatic experiences, but to clear up eschatological questions he appeals to words (1 Th. 4: 15) or disclosed mysteries (1 Cor. 15:51). In 2 Cor. 12:1 "revelations" seems to be the key term (v. 7), and the stress is again on things that Paul heard (v. 4). What the revelations are, Paul does not say, but he does not include the Damascus experience. Paul does not mention the Spirit in this connection. This aspect is plain in Acts 7: 55 when Stephen sees heaven opened and the Son of Man standing at God's right hand. In the life of Yeshua, the only visionary element is in the baptism story, in which he sees the Spirit descending (Mt. 3:16) and hears the voice from heaven (3:17). We have here two sides of common events. On the one side is the assurance that Yeshua is the Divine Son and Messiah; on the other the perceived imparting of the Spirit at the beginning of his ministry as such.

Materially, the revelation by word is primary. The transfiguration is not to be regarded as an ecstatic experience of Yeshua himself. The terms used leave open what form of seeing is intended. Lk. 9: 32 shows that the disciples are awake during the experience. Neither the transfiguration nor the voice is the make of Yeshua himself, so that we might have here a shared visionary process although a real transfiguration is not to be ruled out. The eschatological form and orientation make it unlikely that the transfiguration is an emergence of preexistent glory.

The Resurrection Appearance. We have accounts of resurrection appearances in Mt. 28:9-10, 16; Lk. 24: 13, 36, 50; Jn. 20: 14, 19, 24; Acts 1: 4 and Paul's conversion. The appearances are all isolated, and in Acts 9 3; 22: 6 Yeshua seems to come from heaven. No appearance is said to have occurred during sleep, so the appearances are not dream-visions; Indeed, they do not take place by night. Again, they are always linked with revelations by word. At times the Lord's corporeality is viewed more literally, Lk. 24: 39-40, at times more spiritual, Lk. 24: 36. In 2 Cor. 12: 1 Paul does not include the Damascus experience among his visions (in spite of the optasia of Acts 26: 19; 22: 17-18). If he sees the Lord according to 1 Cor. 9: 1, it is because God reveals his Son to him, Gal. 1: 16. In 1 Cor. 15:3, Paul says that Yeshua "appeared", Lk. 24: 34; Acts 9:17. The stress is on revelation rather than on actual seeing; Yeshua shows himself, and those to whom he does so experience his presence. The Damascus experience is for Paul similar to the prior experiences during the 40 days. The object of the appearances is the risen and exalted Lord, who is there thru the basis of faith and the community. The disciples do not mistake the appearance for the parosia (ressurection). Hence, one should not stress the analogy of the visual element in the two cases. In the case of the Parousia, the important thing is the coming rather than the seeing; the visual element in the appearances, which is stronger, is neither proleptic of eschatological events nor influenced by them.

John 6: 62 does not refer to the ascension as such, but to the exaltation of Yeshua by way of the cross. It thus has in view the spiritual perception that demands decision. When the seeing achieves its goal, it means faith and eternal life, 6: 40. In 16:17, 19, however, the reference is to seeing the earthly life and then the resurrection (or Parousia). Yet in view of the mention of the Spirit this seeing, too, denotes encounter through the Spirit's ministry.

The world does not see Yeshua because it resists the Spirit's work (14: 19). When Yeshua and his disciples are said to see the Father, this seeing cannot be integrated into the usual parallelism of seeing and hearing in John. There is, of course, a distinction between Yeshua' seeing of the Father and the disciples' seeing of the Father, for it is Yeshua himself who reveals the Father to the disciples (12: 45; 14: 9).

Yeshua reveals the Father in a unique way John 12: 45; hence seeing the Father involves submission to His revelation in Yeshua (14:9). Both the historicity of the event and the pre and post-existence of Yeshua are involved. For John seeing is the seeing of faith; indeed, it is faith, although this does not have to mean that it is an anticipation of eschatological seeing. It's more probable significance is that for John verbs of seeing bring out the personal element in the encounter with Yeshua.

Since God is seen in the Son, Jn. 1: 18 is not contesting previous theophanies but simply saying God reveals himself exclusively through the Son. The Son has immediate access to the Father (6: 46); others know God, whether through hearing or seeing, by means of the Son. The point is not that the invisible God becomes visible, but that God reveals himself. 1 Jn. 4:12 maintains the intrinsic invisibility of God. God makes himself known through his works, Rom. 1: 19-20, but supremely through the Son who is his image, Col. 1: 15. At the end, there will still not be direct vision but complete revelation. Future vision will differ from present possibilities (the seeing of 1 Cor. 13: 12 which goes hand in hand with faith), but God is not named in 1 Cor. 13: 12 as the direct object of sight. Vision and sonship are related in Mt. 5: 18 and (eschatologically) in 1 Jn. 3: 2. Vision and sanctification also go hand in hand in these verses, so that the presupposition is full divine likeness (not deification by vision) at the consummation. In a book that is oriented to the visual Rev. 22: 4 also refers to a final seeing of the face of God (and the exhortation in Heb. 12: 14). The NT speaks of the vision of God only with great restraint and in light of the saving revelation of God in Christ. This promise is so unsurpassably great that it is not lightly repeated and thus rings out the more joyfully, as in 1 Jn. 3: 2.

The Apostolic Fathers use verbs of seeing (some 265 instances compared to 170 of hearing) in much the same way as the NT. God sees (1 Clem. 28: 1), but we humans cannot see God except figuratively (Diog. 8. 5-6). We may know God from his visible works (1 Clem. 60.1), and God reveals himself by way of the incarnation because we could not have stood direct vision (Barn. 5.10). Yeshua will be seen at the Parousia, and eschatological fellowship with him is a form of seeing.

Horatos, aoratos, these words, meaning visible and invisible, are important words in Greek philosophy as they become slogans for the sensory world and the world of ideas. Both terms are very rare in the LXX. Horatos means handsome in 2 Sam. 23:21 (and Job 37:21; 34: 26). Aoratos is used in Gen. 1: 2, and we find aoratous in Is. 45: 3, but God is not called aoratos. Philo has horatos over 70 times (often with a negative), and aoratos over 100 times. He adopts and extends the view of Plato. Invisible powers are at work in the cosmos. The nous is invisible, but so especially are God and the divine nature and spirit. Josephus uses aoratos for places that are not, or ought not to be, seen. The soul cannot be seen, but it moves the body. There are no direct rabbinic equivalents for the terms.

The NT uses horatos only in Col. 1: 16 (with aoratos). Ta horatoa here seems to denote the whole earthly sphere, including the stars and other heavenly phenomena, while ta aorata are the heavenly powers which, while created, share God's Invisibility and seek dominion in the human sphere (Eph. 6: 12). Elsewhere aoratos relates only to God. Invisibility is a divine predicate in the doxology in 1 Tim. 1: 17. It is the invisible God who is seen in Heb. 11: 27;

faith enables Moses to accept him as the supreme reality in his demands and promises. Paul in Rom. 1: 20 refers to the invisible nature of God which is manifested in his works. Creation does not make God visible but reveals him. This is also the purpose of Christ as the image of God in 2 Cor. 4:4.

In the Apostolic Fathers, God is invisible in 2 Clem. 20. 5; Diog. 7. 2; Ingnatius Magnesians 3. 2. The earthly life of Yeshua makes visible the preexistent Christ (Ignatius Polycarp 3. 2. In Diog. 6. 4 the invisible soul is guarded by the visible body. Ignatius Polycarp 2.2 makes a distinction between things phenomenal and things invisible, and Ignatius Smyrneans 6. 1 refers to visible and invisible angelic powers.

Horasis, this word means seeing, sight (plural eyes), later "appearance", and in the biblical sphere vision. It is common in the LXX (some 110 times, 38 in Ezekiel and 18 in Daniel) in such senses as sight, appearance, vision. Philo has it over 70 times for the sense or process of sight. He often prefers opsis, as does Josephus. The NT uses it twice for appearance in Rev. 4: 3, and also for vision, Rev. 9: 17; Acts 2: 17; Joel 2:28. In the apostolic fathers, it means eyesight (2 Cam. 1. 6). Spectacle (7. 6), and vision (hermas Visions 2-4).

Horama, this word means "what is to be seen", spectacle, appearance, vision. The LXX used it 43 times, often for vision (Daniel). In the NT, it occurs in Mt. 17: 19 for what the disciples have seen at the transfiguration. In ten instances in Acts (9: 10, 12; 10:3, 17, 19; 11:5; 12: 9; 16: 9-10; 18: 9) it means vision, but often with only formal emphasis on the visionary aspect (9: 10, 12, etc.). In the apostolic fathers, the phrase in Hermas Visions 4.1.3 is reminiscent of 2 Cor. 12:1. The only other examples are in Hermas Visions 3.4 (twice plural; at the night 3.10.6).

Optasia, this noun is an uncommon one. It occurs only four times in the LXX in the sense "appearing" (Esth. 4: 17; Mal. 3: 2). In Lk. 1:22; 24: 23 it refers to angelophanies, and the Damascus appearance is called a heavenly otasia in Acts 26:19. There is little emphasis on the visionary aspect in either Luke or Acts; the stress lies on the revelation by word and the demand for obedience. Paul himself does not use the term for the Damascus incident. In the apostolic fathers Mart. Pol. 5.2 records a vision of Polycarp.

Autoptes, this term has the sense of eyewitness (seeing for oneself). It does not occur in the LXX, but Josephus uses it. The only NT instance is in Lk. 1: 2. Stylistically there are parallels for this, but materially the statement shows that for the tradition it is an inner necessity that eyewitnesses should be mentioned as normative carries.

Epoptes, epopteus, these nouns have such meanings as spectator, observer, then overseer. In the mysteries, it denotes one who comes to have a share in vision. The verb means to view, to inspect, to consider, and in the mysteries to have the rank of an epoptes. The noun occurs in the LXX to indicate that God takes note of things (Esth. 5: 1; 2 Macc. 3: 39), but the verb is not used. Philo used neither noun nor verb, and Josephus has only compounds. The NT uses the verb in 1 Pet. 2:12; 3: 2. Gentiles take note of the conduct of Christians, and when they see their good deeds they will glorify God or be won over. This is no relation here to the use in the mysteries, nor is epoptes in 2 Pet. 1: 16 dependent on this use, for the sense of spectator or observer is adequate enough in context; the specific element of eyewitness is not too strongly emphasized by the word in isolation. God is epoptes in 1 Clem. 59.3 and pantepoptes in 55.6; he sees and knows all human deeds.

Ophthalmos, this word means apple of the eye, eye (mostly plural), and figuratively what is most dear. Many phrases bring out the importance of the eye, and we also find references to seeing with the eyes of the nous or kardia (mind or heart). The LXX uses the word some 700 times, often for human perception or judgment, or for divine perception (Dt. 11: 12).

The eyes can be the seat of evil impulses (Prov. 6: 17; 10: 10; 30: 13; Job 31: 1, 7). Philo uses the word some 130 times, over 100 literally for seeing or sight. He seldom speaks about the eyes of God and mostly uses omma figuratively for the mental eyes. The pseudepigrapha refers to the eyes of God but also say that human eyes may reveal an adulterous or covetous nature. The rabbis, too, speak about evil or good eyes and refer to seeing the seducer in the eye. The NT employs the word some 100 times. As the organ of sight, it occurs in relation to the blind and their healing (also the blinding in Acts 9: 8).

The eyes are heavy in Mt. 26: 43, and tears are wiped off them in Rev. 7: 17. The parable of the mote and the beam (or the speck and the log, Mt. 7: 3) is a warning against judging others. The OT rule of an eye for an eye is quoted in Mt. 5:38, but with an admonition to replace strict justice with love.

The function of the eye is the basis of the image in Mt. 6:22-23, which considers the possibility that the eye might be sound or unsound, with a moral reference. That the eye may entice to sin is stated in 1 Jn. 2:16, and 2 Pet. 2:14. The eye may also be a cause of offense according to Mt. 5:29. Under OT influence, the eye is associated with eyewitness in Mt. 13:16; Lk. 2: 30; 1 Jn. 1:1; Rev. 1: 7.

In connection with the resurrection appearances there is no special singling out of sight (Lk. 24:16, 31; Acts 1: 9); the crucial point is spiritual rather than sensory perception. God grants enlightenment to the eyes of the heart (Acts 26: 18; 1 Jn. 2: 11; Eph. 1: 18). Only rarely does NT refer to the eyes of God (1 Pet. 3: 12; Heb. 4: 13).

In the apostolic fathers ophthalmos is rare except for ten references in 1 Clement. The Martyrdom of Polycarp applies "eyes of the heart" to martyrs. 1 Cor. 2: 9 is quoted in 1 Clem. 34.8; 2 Clem. 11.7; Mart. Pol. 2: 3. Ommata occurs only in 1 Clem. 19.3.

Kathorao, this word means to look down, then more generally "to view", and figuratively "to perceive", to note, to look over, to give attention to. The LXX uses Kathorao four times and kateidon four times, usually for sense perception, or anthropomorphically for God's looking down from heaven (Job 10;4). Philo uses kathorao 34 times with a greater emphasis on intellectual perception, as is shown by the objects, by the fact that God may be the subject, and by the link with dianoia (although not with nous). In Josephus, on the other hand, sense perception is mostly at issue, although we also find the transferred meaning to perceive, to inspect. The only NT used of Kathorao is in Rom. 1: 20. Since the construction here rules out sense perception prior to intellectual apprehension, what seems to be meant is sense perception that is at the same time apprehension (noumena kathoratai). Hence, the poiemata are not just empirical phenomena but phenomena or processes that must be considered in a way that combines sensory and intellectual perception, e.g., God's works in history. The context seems to make it plain that true perception of these is not a possibility that is naturally available to sinners (v. 19); it depends on the divine action in self-revelation. This is no less necessary at the level of general revelation than special revelation.

Proorao, proeiden, this word means "to see before", ahead, earlier, in advance, and hence "to provide for". The middle means "to have before one's eyes", to have seen in advance (God's advance knowledge of human ways and deeds. Philo uses the term for foreseeing the future. This is possible for God but not for us. Josephus agrees, except in the case of the prophets, but he also uses the term for foreseeing and taking precautions against dangers. In the NT Acts 2: 31 says that David as a prophet has advance knowledge of the resurrection of Yeshua. Acts 2: 25 quotes Ps. 16: 8 to the same effect. The meaning in Acts 21:29 is "to have seen earlier". Gal. 3: 8 refers to the foreseeing of Scripture. Problepomai has the same sense of foreseeing in Heb. 11:40, with God as subject. In the apostolic fathers, the sense in Ignatius Trallians 8.1 is that of foreseeing dangers and taking precautions against them.

In concluding Contemplation, we find that it points to a conjuring of a sight or vision of nature, that wasn't previously known or observable. Since we fell from Absolute Awareness, this manifesting of subjective ideals became a necessity, in combination with our worship, of man to elevate towards that which is greater than ourselves. We have to continually view what's moral and unbiased in the scriptures and teachings in order for the explanation, practice, and reward, to be had, can come through. This is done through the focal consciousness and determination of will in contemplation.

Contemplation kept up very near to what we were created for ultimately. But, just like meditation, became a lost art in this physical world and a lost skill to this world, and so that brought us to prayer. Prayer is thought to be the fix all cure all, but let's see what it truly is through an investigation into it. Let's see what it fixes, if anything, and what it cures, if at all.

Prayer is a part of meditation, a portion of contemplation. All of the major, population controlling, belief systems have a form of prayer in them, and they have been teaching and requiring prayer for the better part of a millennium. But as an observation is made, it becomes clear that something more than just prayer is needed to fix Our problems, illnesses, and dis-eases. Prayer is a great starter in this healing process, but what it is not is the panacea of life's roles. You be the judge.

Here, in this Addendum on Coalescing Knowledge, as it pertains to Worship, Prayer, Meditation, and Contemplation, We have given explanations, definitions, Greek terms and meanings, from their earliest expositions, and some commentaries and Church Father's teachings concerning these subjects. We have shown a vastness in the true Exploration of Overstanding an important factor in the lives of such Ones who deem a Great Value to these components of Spirituality. Now comes Application.

How high, how far, or how deep this information can take Us is dependent on how much of it We can cause to Coalesce in Our Daily Lives. The scriptural references bring in the scenario perspective of how each element can be applied. Life experiences will create the opportunities necessary for practice, and Our Will's Strength will implement whatever level of Ability that can be conjured up in Us. This is how a subject is used for Coalescing Knowledge. This is why "What Do You Know: Is it Real?" is not just a book title, but an actual question that We think needs to be juxtaposed with other concerns of necessities described by religion, politics, and psychology; like in Maslow's Hierarchy of Needs Pyramid. We used Maslow's Hierarchy as an objective instructor, one of many, that We can use all or some of to refurbish ideals, beliefs, and perspectives; in order to overstand "More" concerning "Why Are We Here". And just like discovering a psychological system that fits Our needs, a religious and political system will need to be discovered for our use also. So Ask The Question.

Epilogue

There is a knowledge and degree of ability required to have a sense perception of what the Sacred Scripts have in wait for Us. We are not as familiar with the Greek, Roman and Semitic words, terms, and definitions that allow for a fuller understanding of those Precious and Holy Books. Even in the Original Translation text of the Bible and Quran, in English, there is a "lost in translation" meaning that is obfuscated for us in this language.

We need to possess the correct reference materials that give Us assistance in Our complete study of Life from a Socio-Religious perspective. We know that being Studious is an attitude that seems to be lost in today's society, but, none-the-less, it is required since the writers and compilers of our Sacred Scripts were Studious and Diligent in preparing and delivering them to Us.

Remembering that the Greeks and Romans had a need to "Anthropomorphize" all Gnostic and Esoteric Information, sheds light on Our need to reverse this process; in order to discover an Origin and Truth to what We seek to know of this world. That means that all components, elements terms, and phrases, need description, definition and explanation as to what they really are.

Once this Understanding is gained, and can be applied as Wisdom, We can ask a Most Important Question of Our

Doctrines, Symbols, Rituals and Ways of Life, and that is "Is it Religion"?

GLOSSARY

Subjective - of, relating to, or determined by the mind, ego or consciousness as the subject of experience and knowledge.

Noumenon - an object that is conceived by reason and consequently thinkable but is not knowledge by the senses: An object of purely intellectual institution as opposed to an object of sensuous perception. Noumena, Pl.

Homogeneous - of a similar kind or nature: comparable, equivalent; having no discordant elements: consistent, compatible.

Psychological - relating to, characteristic of, directed towards, influencing, arising in, or acting through the mind.

Hedonism - An ethical doctrine taught by the ancient Epicureans and Cyrenaics and by the modern utilitarians that assert that pleasure and happiness is the sole chief good of life.

Physiognomy - the technique or art of discovering temperament and character from outward appearance (as from facial features) 2a: The facial feature that shows the quality of mind or character by peculiarities of configuration or cast or characteristic expression: inner character or quality as revealed outwardly.

***Homousian*-** of the same substance.

***Homotousion*-** of like substance

***Worship*-** the reverence or veneration tendered a divine being or supernatural power; an act, process, or instance of expressing such veneration by performing or taking part in religious exercises or ritual; respect, admiration, or devotion for an object or esteem.

***Veneration*-** a feeling of respect mingled with awe excited by the dignity, wisdom, or superiority of a person, by hollowed association: the act of admiring humbly and respectfully esp. by the expressing of deeply reverent feeling; The phrenologic faculty of reverence.

***Phrenologic*-** Phren = Mind (Diaphragm = to enclose) mental.

Ology = a branch of knowledge

Ic -having the character or form of: being; consisting of; relating to, derived from, or containing; in the manner of; like that of, characteristic of, associated or dealing with, exhibiting, affected with, caused by.

***Worship*-** ME = n archaic- dignity, importance; a person of standing or importance, worthiness, respect, reverence paid to a divine being. A form of religious practice with its creed and ritual; extravagant respect or admiration for or devotion to an object of esteem.

***Revere*-** L revereri- re-against + vereri- to fear, respect. + to show devoted deferential honor to; to honor and admire profoundly and respectfully. Revere stresses deference and tenderness of feelings. Reverence presupposed an intrinsic merit and inviolability in the one honored and corresponding depth of feeling in the one honoring.

***Intrinsic*-** internal, inwardly + belonging to the essential nature of constitution of a thing.

***Inviolability*-** secure from violation or profanation; unassailable, inviolable, incapable of being broken or destroyed; incorruptible, sacrosanct = most holy.

***Unassailable*-** not liable to doubt, attack, or question. Not responsible, obligated, or able to incur doubt.

***Deferential*-** showing or expressing deference: Deference = the act or attitude of differing- a yielding of judgment or preference out of respect for the position, wish, or known opinion of another.

Defer- to bring down, bring, carry, to refer or submit for determination or decision: To submit or yield through authority, respect, force, awe, propriety.

Propriety = peculiar, proper, or true nature, character, or condition; quality or trait.

Ras Jah Strength

Solomon & Makeda Publishing Presents...

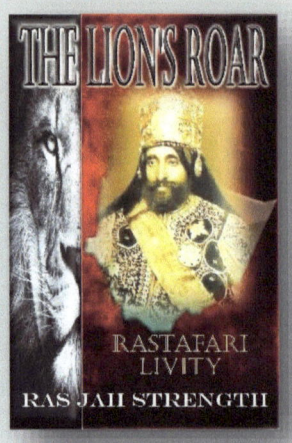

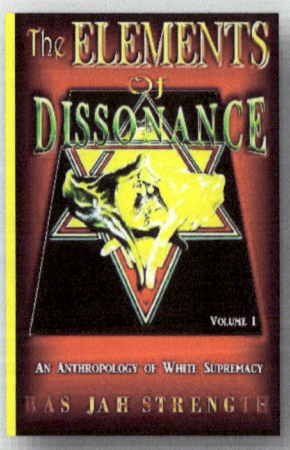

If You Are Interested In Writing And Publishing With <u>Solomon & Makeda Publishing</u>, Visit Us At <u>WWW.SM4PUBLISHING.COM</u> Today And We Will Show You How!

www.ingramcontent.com/pod-product-compliance
Lightning Source LLC
Chambersburg PA
CBHW041805160426
43191CB00004B/56